# NOT **ONE** SHRINE

# NOT **ONE** SHRINE

## TWO FOOD WRITERS DEVOUR TOKYO

BECKY SELENGUT & MATTHEW AMSTER-BURTON

**ILLUSTRATIONS BY DENISE SAKAKI**

Version 1.0.8, 4 December 2016

Illustrated by Denise Sakaki
Cover design by Denise Sakaki
Book design by Matthew Amster-Burton and
Denise Sakaki

# TABLE OF CONTENTS

# INTRODUCTION

## BECKY

I was standing in my tiny Seattle kitchen looking out at a gray sky, running my fingers idly back and forth over the latch on the window. My grandmother had recently died and I was wanting to travel, out of my body preferably, but out of the country would do. I needed something to look forward to, and being a lover of Japanese cuisine, Japan has always been on my list. "Can I go with you next time?" My words hit the phone before I realized they sounded a bit desperate. "Ha ha, I mean, you know, theoretically."

"Sure," he said, "I hate traveling alone."

And that was that.

I met Matthew eight years ago. I had cooked a fancy multi-course dinner party with a pastry chef friend at a secret dinner club. He was one of the guests, a food writer whose name I recognized from his columns. Since that dinner, we've connected in a way that can only be described as sibling-esque. We're linked by our love of food, humor, and a mutual butt-clenching fear of heights. Soon we formed a writing group. The members included me. And him. We took an improv class together and once we finished that we challenged ourselves to perform stand-up at a brutal open-mic night in front of a hostile crowd. We launched a comedy podcast where—so goes our tagline—we combine our neuroses like Jewish Supertwins.

So, yeah, we got along well. But that's in the context of our lives, where we go home every night to our families, see each other once or twice a week. Text each other when we see something funny. Sharing an apartment in Japan, I might see his underwear. I'm not sure if he's a boxers or briefs guy and—BLARGH—I don't want to know.

I've traveled a bunch in my life, more rugged travel in my twenties that found me straddling chickens on a bus in Guatemala with 10 hours left to go on some godforsaken highway in the middle of nowhere, little white paper barf bags shoved into the cracks of the windows for the millions of stomach-churning curves. I slept under mosquito netting in cheap roach- and gecko-populated motel rooms in rural Thailand and drank milky moonshine distilled from agave on the side of a dusty road in Chiapas, Mexico. My thirties found me more comfortably touring Italy, France, and Argentina, via rented cars and apartments, drinking moderately-priced bottles of red wine. Now that I'm in my forties, my rugged days are firmly behind me. I've also learned the importance of not stretching myself too thin. Save energy, cut plans in half, find a home base and branch out from there. Matthew was on the same page.

We rented a two-bedroom apartment in Tokyo through Airbnb. We wouldn't leave the city for the week we'd be there. There would be no tours of shrines. No museums. We were there to devour Tokyo.

We had to remain focused.

NOODLES
Candy!
BOOZE!
BECKY
MATTHEW
bento

## MATTHEW

Why did I want to go to Japan with Becky? Probably to prove to myself that I'm not crazy.

I fell into a relationship with Japan in 2010, when my daughter Iris and I spent a week in Tokyo for spring break. We spoke no Japanese and got around via the international language of hand gestures and plastic food.

Since then I've been to Japan three more times. I've studied Japanese, read it pretty well, and speak it pretty badly. So when Becky mentioned to me that she was thinking about a trip to Japan, I said, "Sure, I'll come along and translate and tell you where to eat."

Then my burlap sack of Jewish anxieties popped open, and out came the flying monkeys of the mental apocalypse.

- Wait, I can't actually speak Japanese at the kindergarten level yet. In fact, kids in Japan always laugh at me when I try to talk to them. It must be hilarious meeting a grownup who talks like a baby.

- Becky is allergic to raw onions and garlic. There isn't a lot of garlic in Japanese food, but when there is, it's probably enough to kill her. Raw green onions are everywhere. If I got Becky killed in Japan, where would my trial be held?

- Becky is a professional chef. I'm a home cook who's happy to eat $5 Seattle teriyaki for lunch on a regular basis. What if we can't agree on what to eat?

And above all:

- You know, I think Japan is pretty great, but Becky is probably a more experienced traveler than me. What if she thinks Tokyo is boring, Westernized, and sterile?

I've romanticized Japan to a humiliating degree. In 2012, I spent July in a tiny Tokyo apartment with my wife and daughter and wrote a whole book about the experience. The book can be summarized as follows: Tokyo has a jillion really good, cheap restaurants, and people who work in stores are nice to you. Repeat for 60,000 words. Also, I failed to include addresses for most of the restaurants I mentioned. It's like a guidebook with the useful pages ripped out.

So it was an absolute shock when my book became a bestseller in Japan. Yes, I'm bragging, but I still don't understand why anyone in Japan would want to read it, except that I guess it's nice to have some guy say positive things about you and your country. My next book will be called *Indonesians Are Outrageously Attractive.* I've never been to Indonesia, but I know a quarter of a billion people live there. Maybe half of them would buy my book?

The trick with falling in love with a place or a person is getting your friends on board. This was my big question. Introducing Becky to Japan was basically like saying, "Hey, you know how I've been raving about this new person I'm dating? Well, here she is! What do you think?"

Becky is the least bullshit-tolerant person I know. Would she say, "Yeah, uh, we need to talk"?

Only one way to find out. A week before Thanksgiving, Becky and I hopped onto an ANA 787, nonstop from Seattle to Tokyo.

# UP IN THE AIR

## MATTHEW

This was my first time flying ANA, one of Japan's two national airlines. The name stands for All Nippon Airways, which couldn't sound more '80s if they changed it to Culture Club Legwarmer Airlines. Remember how Americans were afraid of Japanese businessmen in the '80s? Can we pretend that never happened?

ANA's trans-Pacific flights are notable for a few features in addition to a general atmosphere of non-suckiness. In no particular order:

- Instead of window shades, the Plexiglas itself can be brightened and dimmed via magic.

- The in-flight entertainment system features seat-to-seat messaging. This was handy, since Becky and I weren't sitting together. The interface is slow and clunky and prone to more typos than the crankiest iPhone. I really want to eavesdrop on drunken airplane sexts, which I assume is the main use of this feature. You can also assign yourself a nickname. Mine was Pulpo (octopus in Spanish). Becky's was Tako (octopus in Japanese). I neglected to test how dirty you can make the nicknames before the computer folds its arms and refuses. I apologize to our readers and promise to make this my first priority next time. Yours truly, MegaCock69.

Later, someone told me that the magic windows and crappy SMS system aren't particular to ANA. Fine. But I bet you won't find the next two items on Delta.

- ANA's signature nonalcoholic beverage is Aromatic Kabosu Juice. Kabosu is a little Japanese citrus fruit, kind of like a cross between a lime and a mandarin orange. The juice is amazing. They will mix it with vodka on request.

- In first and business class, you can get ramen. We were not in first or business class, but we had to walk past it. Fuck those guys.

That said, the food in coach is great. Like, I would eat this food outside a plane. For dinner we had miso-simmered mackerel with root vegetables, rice, soba noodles, and melon and pineapple with actual flavor. And green tea.

So I ate mackerel, drank kabosu juice, stabbed ineffectively at my screen, and took a nap. Then we were in

Japan.

Here's what I wish someone would invent: a plane that lands safely at your hotel, to avoid that horrible feeling of *I just landed and now I have to buy another ticket and get on another form of transportation and I JUST WANT A MATTRESS.* Yes, I'm familiar with airport hotels, which are great if you're looking to sleep with pharmacists at a convention. I don't know why this is just occurring to me now, but just how fucked up do people get at a pharmacist convention? Like, probably enough to make Studio 54 look like kindergarten, right?

Anyway, we got on the train into the city, and as we approached central Tokyo, I must have looked pretty happy, because Becky turned to me and said, "You really like it here, don't you?" I do, but also I was daydreaming about crashing a pharmacist convention.

## BECKY ✿

I flew ANA to Bangkok back in 1999. I had just graduated from culinary school and it was my big trip to celebrate all the hard work. I was going to eat my body weight in unidentifiable Thai treats wrapped in banana leaves and boat loads of curry. The Bacchanalian feast started on the plane. I have never forgotten the bento box those lovely flight attendants served me on that flight.

Fifteen years later, while the rest of the airline industry went from "Some frills" to "No frills" to "That will be $45 for three peanuts and an oxygenated cabin," ANA kept handing out comforting hot towels, green tea, artistically arranged bento boxes and are-you-kidding-me free cups of goddamn Häagen-Dazs. "Japan is awesome," I said to the guy in 23B, even though, at the time, "Japan" was technically "flying over Meyers Chuck, Alaska."

I got on Seat-to-Seat Messaging™ to tell Matthew how excited I was about the ice cream and got the following cryptic message: "Hlp. Cme to seat. Dropped can't fnd." He had dropped his glasses and in his sleeping pill–addled state couldn't locate them. A helpful ANA flight attendant found them for him. I sat up in my chair and looked over to the right side of the plane. Matthew was slumped towards the tinted Night-Mode windows, asleep, dreaming Ambien dreams of the Tokyo skyline.

Almost there.

# GOING COMMANDO

## BECKY ✿

Beating jet lag is all about mastering the first night. The trick is to harness great gobs of internal fortitude to stay awake until bedtime, no matter what time you arrive. Follow these rules carefully:

- No hot showers, no hot baths. Taking a long, hot shower is a nice idea, but not today (and taking a long, hot bath is an express, one-way ticket to Snoozeville).

- No napping. Don't even hit the proverbial futon before it's the exact moment you want to pass out.

- No booze. Alcohol is not your friend unless you're a professional drinker.

- Stay sober, alert, and dirty. SAD, for short. I worked long and hard on that acronym. You're welcome.

But let's back up, shall we? At Narita Airport, Matthew and I shook hands on a gentleman's bet as to who could make it past 9 p.m. The gauntlet thrown, I mentally plotted out the rest of the day so it involved lots of movement. If you keep moving, it's much harder to slip into a narcoleptic state, though not entirely impossible. Matthew had reserved us one night at a *ryokan* (traditional inn). We checked into the Ryokan Shigetsu in Asakusa, shed our bags, tested the firmness of the tatami mat and futon (firm and semi-firm, respectively), pondered the complimentary green tea and sesame seed confections, and headed immediately back onto the streets. I was thrilled to be in Japan for the first time and 99 percent comatose. It was 4:08 p.m.

Matthew will perhaps have a greater sense of the details of this first night. What I can remember is this: We walked by a very famous temple with a big lantern-thingy and a large gate. I think it was called the Thunder Dome. No, the Thunder Gate. Yes, that. We ate in a tiny restaurant. The food was good (tempura, *karaage* fried chicken, miso soup). The ice-cold beer was incredible, but a mistake. I noticed, too late, that he didn't order a beer, that sneaky rat bastard. I started yawning great big dramatic, room-sucking yawns in an attempt to bring him down faster. Back on the streets, we passed endless artisan *senbei* (rice cracker) stalls. My eyes were tearing up, I was so tired. It was 6:46 p.m.

Matthew suggested we head back to the inn, put on

our *yukata* (robes) and slippers and hit the top-floor baths. Upon arrival, the host had pressed into my hand the English language playbook on using *onsen* (a traditional Japanese bath). It had lots of cartoon clipart of pudgy white people with X's through them. I will paraphrase: Don't be an idiot. Wear your yukata to the bath. Don't wear your yukata into the bath. Clean yourself at the shower stall before entering. Don't wash your junk in the bath. Okay, it didn't say the last bit, but maybe it should have. It's probably a good idea to spell things out for sleep-deprived foreigners.

It's customary to tie the yukata above the waist if you're a woman and below the waist if you're a man and somewhere in between if you're not sure. In the inn, you can wear them to meals, to the baths, and even to bed. The left side of the yukata goes over the right side, unless you're attending your own funeral. The *obi* (belt) brings it all together. There were other rules but I was too bleary-eyed to keep reading. The beer made me painfully tired and Matthew was waiting for me in the hall. I tried not to laugh out loud at us in our traditional robes, looking to the world like gangly extras in the never-released Jewish version of James Clavell's Shōgun. Once upstairs, I slipped into the hot water in the large wooden tub in the women's bath and looked out the window at the glow of Tokyo's skyline. I had the place all to myself. I love that early-on vacation moment when you shed that first layer of travel weariness; your shoulders relax, you let out a long, contented sigh and close your eyes.

WAKE UP! 7:38 p.m. I headed back to my room and

puttered around. Don't lie down, I said to myself. Don't do it. But let's be real for a second, in a teeny-tiny Japanese ryokan room, if you're not sitting on the toilet, you're laying on the tatami mat—there is simply no other real estate to explore and no chairs, so fuck it. I lay down and began reading books on Japanese culture and food. The next thing I knew, I was awakened by a text from Matthew: "are you still awake?" 8:44 p.m.

Goddammit, I lost.

I tried to go back to sleep even though my normal bedtime is midnight, because who really cares now? After all, fighting jet lag is not about being refreshed, it's about winning. Three hours later—BLAM—wide awake. I clicked on the light, grabbed the bath etiquette pamphlet and read some more. Wait, what was that bit there? "Remember to wear your underwear under your yukata."

Oops.

## MATTHEW

I win! BOO-YA.

Now that I think about it, Becky, remember how the bet was for $1,000? You were kind of sleepy, but we definitely shook on it. Also, remember the part where Robert Redford offered you a million dollars to...wait, maybe I'm thinking of something else.

If you've never been to Japan, you've probably heard it described as "Westernized." The person saying this is typically a guy who got burned out after teaching English in Japan in his 20s. He makes the accusation in the tone you'd use to lament that an old friend joined a weird religion. Just not the same anymore.

If you're planning your first trip to Japan, go ahead and assume that this is right, that after marinating in Euro-American influence since Matthew Perry and David Schwimmer arrived in 1853, Japan is now the 51st state plus a sprinkle of soy sauce. That way, it'll be more fun when you arrive and your head explodes from how wrong the idea is.

Like a lot of nonsense, there's a sliver of truth to the claim. Japan enthusiastically hoovers up international culture—from Asia, from Europe, and especially from the U.S. It has over 3,000 McDonald's outlets, over 1,000 Starbucks, and over 500 Denny's. You can get a bucket at KFC or a delivery (on a tiny scooter) from Domino's or Pizza Hut. Road and transit signs are in Japanese and English. Sportcoats outnumber kimonos fifty to one.

All of that is true, but it completely misses the point. When you first visit a Japanese shrine (not that we did), you expect every aspect of the experience to be new and different. When do I bow? How many times do I clap? Why is this guy with a camera asking me to disrobe?

When you go to a Japanese Pizza Hut or Denny's, you're probably expecting a carbon copy of the chain you grew up with. During breakfast at a Denny's in Tokyo, however, I once watched an American open the menu, frown at the fermented soybeans and tofu salad, and say to his family, "What the fuck is this?" Pizza Hut serves pies like Melted Beef Stew, Bulgogi, or a $38 alternative to the Meat Lover's®: Iberico ham.

My point is not that you should order Pizza Hut in Japan, although I know you want some melted beef stew up in your stewhole. Actually, I have two points:

- A Westerner who comes to Japan will be continuously surprised, amused, and bewildered by local customs and preferences, despite (and because of!) the presence of lots of Western stuff.

- Japanese cities—especially Tokyo—are so big and packed with stuff that a thousand Starbucks are barely noticeable. You will never, ever wind up in a situation in Japan where you're stuck eating American fast food. And if you do, you'll probably get a hell of a story out of it.

One of the more obvious cultural differences between the U.S. and Japan is that people here love to take baths and don't mind sharing the bath with strangers. I mean, don't show up at a random house and jump into the tub with whoever's in there. That's frowned upon except in certain rural prefectures.

When you arrive at a Japanese-style hotel or inn (even one of those capsule hotels), the staff will almost always tell you where the public bath is. Don't be a fool: get in the pool. Or the bath. Whatever.

Now, having said that, I can usually handle about ten minutes in the bath. If you go to the bath with friends of the same sex, you can hang around and chat with them. Naked. Otherwise, you have to split up and yell at each other over the divider between the men's and women's sections. Coed bathing used to be common in Japan, but is no longer. Total crime against humanity, right?

No one else was using the Shigetsu's bath when Becky and I arrived, so I showered off and got into the cedar-lined tub. The water was at a gentle poaching temperature. I enjoyed the view of the Tokyo Skytree observation tower. I tried to think deep philosophical thoughts, like Jack Handey. What makes Japan unique? Would I eat whale meat just to freak out Becky? What is melted beef stew? What if some ladies came in here accidentally?

Five minutes of deep thoughts was plenty, so I went back to my room and played video games.

## BECKY ✿

Allow me to step back into the lukewarm bath water here. While Matthew was playing video games and I was still marinating in the tub upstairs, I was thinking about the whole bathing thing and well, where he has a five minute max poaching time, this bird takes at least 45 minutes to fully cook. And beyond that, I knew I wasn't fully experiencing all that a Japanese onsen can deliver because I was alone in my tub, it was sort of small, and the "NO" drawings of pudgy, cartoon white people meant that I didn't make any totally embarrassing, publicly-witnessed cultural mistakes. Where's the fun in that?

I asked Matthew to take me to a real onsen, one where I'd be guaranteed to screw up. A few days later, we took a long train ride out to the Utsukushii no Yu onsen. We walked in, took off our shoes, and Matthew expertly navigated the ticket vending machine to get us access to the baths. We placed our shoes in lockers by the door, grabbed our locker keys, and walked up to the counter. While Matthew was handing over his tickets, I saw a small sign that read "No tattoos." I poked Matthew's arm and pointed out my small, three-inch-wide tattoo of a rosemary branch on my upper back. And that's when the needle came off the record.

## MATTHEW

I knew Becky would expose herself to me sooner or later.

Seriously, I felt like a real jerk. I knew Japanese baths didn't allow tattoos and totally forgot that Becky had one. The reason tattoos are banned is kind of crazy: They're associated with the Japanese gangsters known as *yakuza*. These guys are known for their elaborate full-body tattoos.

Now, I realize Becky is probably a member of an international lesbian crime syndicate (which is about the most entertaining phrase I can imagine), and I know this comes dangerously close to calling for racial profiling, but would it really mean the end of civil society to let a white girl's culinary tattoo slip into your bathhouse?

So, no bath for us. Instead, we went next door to Mister Donut. Mister Donut is a wildly inventive chain that sells crackly-topped crème brûlée doughnuts, a Cronut knockoff series, and extra-stretchy mochi-infused doughnuts. I deferred to Becky on the choice so she could drown her sorrows in sugar. She bought each of us a Pon de Ring, a confection made up entirely of doughnut holes strung together like beads on a necklace.

"Sorry about the bath," I said. But she was already chewing her way to blissful relaxation.

# RED FLAGS

## MATTHEW

"Hey, Becky," I asked while we were planning our trip, "what neighborhood do you want to stay in? Shibuya? Kichijōji? Takadanobaba?"

"I've got an idea," she replied. "How about you decide?"

We scrutinized Airbnb listings and decided on a two-bedroom in Takadanobaba, a name that means something like "high rice field horse-training ground." The neighborhood currently found there has absolutely none of these qualities, but it's every bit as entertaining in its own way as if mighty steeds were galloping around, trampling rice seedlings.

On our check-in date, we came out of the west exit of Takadanobaba Station, crossed the main street, and entered a narrow street with an arched sign over it. The sign said SAKAE-DŌRI (Prosperity Street) in Japanese, and the street was maybe three blocks long. Most of the other people we saw were obviously students at one of the many nearby colleges (Tokyo Fuji University, Waseda University, Gakushuin Women's College, and so on), no doubt looking for the same things as college students everywhere: cheap food and someone to share it with. We saw plenty of couples making googly eyes at each other, and you could almost smell the hookup-inducing pheromones, so I offered to bet Becky $200 that we would never see a Japanese couple engaging in PDA. Since this was my fifth time in Japan and I'd never seen so much as a kiss on the cheek, she smugly refused to take the bet.

Me, I was ogling restaurants, which were emitting plenty of mouthwatering pheromones themselves. I counted thirty before we got to the end of the first block. Conveyor-belt sushi. Non-conveyor-belt sushi. Ramen. Udon. *Yakiniku* (Korean-style grilled meat). A Turkish restaurant. Tonkatsu. Student hangouts serving cheap beer and small plates. Girlie bars like Girls Bar Juicy and Club Jelly. A perplexing restaurant offering HOME MADE PIZZA and FUNKY JUNKIE MIX FOOD. Down a narrow side alley, the savory pancake called *okonomiyaki*.

My stomach was growling for some Funky Junkie, but we still needed to check into our apartment. Past the west end of Sakae-dōri, we crossed a canal and went by the entrance to Tokyo Fuji University. We walked past a shabu-shabu restaurant and a cozy-looking sushi bar and found our building perched on the edge of the canal. Trees were dropping autumn leaves into the water, and the leaves collected along the edges like painted curbs. From our seventh floor balcony, we had a view of two massive backhoes on a construction site, each machine painted pink with white polka dots. I'm not sure which mental image I enjoy more: Burly construction guys digging with pink backhoes, or sexy construction ladies doing the same. Maybe one of each? I bet this exists on the internet.

We went back out into the urban jambalaya of Sakae-dōri, and I asked Becky what she wanted for lunch. She must have some kind of Inigo Montoya "Father, guide my sword" relationship with her stomach, because she said, "Yakitori," right away.

"Hmm," I replied. A lot of yakitori places are only open for dinner. This was the case for the first two we peeked into. Yakitori is generally cheap drinking food. You might get takeout skewers from a supermarket at lunchtime, but I couldn't remember ever having it for lunch in a restaurant. Once I went to a semi-famous yakitori place in Roppongi, only to find that they don't serve chicken at lunch, only grilled beef tongue, and not even on sticks. (It was good, though!)

So I was worried we might not find a yakitori place, and then I'd have to figure out what to eat instead—and my stomach is no Inigo Montoya. Then we came across Sumire.

By American restaurant standards, Sumire was throwing red flags like a bullfighter. Among the warning signs:

- The place was open for lunch when none of its

neighbors were. Desperation?

- The restaurant was large and empty.
- The menu had glossy photos and too many different kinds of food. In addition to yakitori, the restaurant served fried stuff, salads, hot pots, and grilled beef (most yakitori places stick to chicken, vegetables, and occasionally pork).

Basically, we're talking a deserted Applebee's.

How was it? Let me ask Becky.

### BECKY ✿

What Matthew pointed out, namely that this place "was throwing red flags like a bullfighter," is absolutely true. Every part of me did not want to eat there. Spoiler alert: it was great.

As an American, you implicitly understand some things about American restaurants, and a big one—really the only significant one—is that if a street is hopping with life and there are people enjoying food in all of the restaurants around you but one, it's for a good reason. Ignore that at your own peril. Here are a couple plausible reasons that a restaurant in the U.S. would be empty at dinnertime on a bustling street humming with people.

1. The cook has a small heroin problem. The last two diners waited for three days, four hours and 35 minutes for their first course and when it came

out, it was served off the backside of his trashed ex-girlfriend.

2. The health department came by, closed the place down because there were no hand washing facilities, and rat poison was found on the same shelf as the grade F hamburger meat. It just reopened. You're the first customer.

3. The owner just backed out because he's now philosophically opposed to brick-and-mortar operations (i.e. he's broke). From here on out, he's hosting pop-ups only.

But we're in Japan and we can't put on our American hats and decide that, no doubt about it, this place is empty because the food sucks, it's a drug front, or we will contract Hep B if we eat the lettuce. Why was it completely empty? I have no idea, but when Matthew said "here!" and pointed to the empty, too brightly lit place with servers and cooks who appeared to be 17 years old, I looked at him like he had asked me to ride bareback on a pig down the middle of the street. *Dude,* I thought, *an appetite is a terrible thing to waste. I only get hungry a limited number of times a day. Do not waste my space.*

I said nothing. Look, he's been in Japan five times—he knows a lot about Japanese food. Against my better judgment, I had to trust the guy.

We ordered a bunch of stuff, and by we, I mean Matthew, because this was my first full day and despite studying the language for six months, I spoke Japanese like a drunk toddler with a lisp. Out came the shishitos, those lovely mild green Russian roulette peppers where one out of 10 might blow your head off; a small plate of crispy, sweet and floral pickled cucumber rounds; perfectly cooked and luscious young chicken with skin; juicy and smoky pieces of Wagyu sirloin on skewers; a tempura fried chicken thing which was just okay and two ginger sodas.

The food was, save for the tempura thing, excellent. Excellent and affordable and fast. High quality fast food that includes vegetables? Wake up, America, we're doing it wrong.

And here's my theory, thank you for asking: Commodity food in America short-shrifts the back end of the ingredients and adds necessary complexity to the front end to make up for it. The U.S. grows our food with a single goal: Let it be cheap. That goal makes for a lot of terrible practices that you can taste in the ingredients. Starting with poor ingredients necessitates lots of creativity and seasonings to turn it into something edible. As Shakespeare once said, "with ample spices, you can twist a turd into a curry, but at the end of the day, it's still a curried turd." Or something like that.

There's a farm in Washington state called Mair Farm-Taki. It's run by Japanese-American farmers and they focus on only a handful of crops each season, growing them organically and with great care and focus. Each and every last vegetable I've eaten from this farm is a thing of magnificent beauty. When I buy a cucumber or daikon radish or kabocha squash from these guys, I do the bare minimum to it before it's eaten. To do a bunch of complex and fancy maneuvering would negate the investment of effort put into the back end of the ingredient. If an ingredient could talk, it would be saying "step aside chef and give me the mic." This is just one of the reasons why I think deserted Japanese restaurants that would give Americans the heebie-jeebies can serve great food.

But if the bathrooms are disgusting, don't ever go back.

## MATTHEW

Later that evening, we went out for a walk, and I squinted at the name of a bustling, well-lit Chinese restaurant a couple blocks from our apartment. "I wonder why this place is so popular," I said. "Oh, I get it. It's an all-you-can-eat, all-you-can-drink place."

Yes, all-you-can-drink is a thing in Japan, which may explain why the previously quiet street was now packed with a thousand college students blitzed out of their minds. Including, yes, a couple engaged in a spirited face-sucking session on the bridge over the canal. Becky, you should have taken the bet.

# DOING TIME DOWN UNDER

## BECKY ✿

I helped Matthew edit his book *Pretty Good Number One: An American Family Eats Tokyo* back when I knew very little about the city. What I thought I knew about Tokyo was this: huge, crushing crowds; Bill Murray from the movie Lost in Translation; neon everywhere; high-fashion high school girls wearing cat ears, mini skirts, and crazy boots; karaoke; the movie Tampopo; geisha. So yeah, I knew nothing more than half-truths and vague stereotypes regurgitated to me via Hollywood.

In his book, Matthew talked about visiting *depachika,* the basement floor of department stores dedicated to lavish displays of Japanese food and drink. I imagined it as a sort of Filene's Basement farmers market with sale bins of ramen noodles, instant dashi and chopsticks. Not that he described it that way. But I couldn't get my head around the idea of museum-quality displays of the finest food in the world in the basement of a department store. With samples.

Matthew decided to take an introvert's day off, so I headed out on my own to Takashimaya, a depachika right on the subway line. I stepped through the doors and was rendered speechless. Mouth agape, it was clear I had arrived at the single most amazing way to experience Japanese food in one fell swoop. No book, not his, not this one, can possibly prepare the food professional or food lover for a Tokyo depachika. It's one of those things you have to see to believe.

You know in Willy Wonka and the Chocolate Factory when they are in that rainbow-colored garden and everything is edible? Remember, too, when greedy Augustus Gloop falls into the chocolate river and gets sucked up a tube? Wonka stands passively by, munching on an edible teacup, while the kids freak out at Augustus' girth stuck in the tube, the pressure of the chocolate river building beneath him. Wonka's seen this kind of bad behavior before—he just blows his whistle and the Oompa-Loompas go clean up the mess. I wanted to hurl myself at every display in the depachika with the abandon of Augustus Gloop. I wanted to find Ramen River and get sucked up a tube of shōyu broth. Surely, it would go somewhere amazing. Somewhere amazing with lots of fatty pork.

Instead, I took a ridiculous number of photos. Photos of two-foot tall displays of *daigaku imo* (sugar-glistening shellacked sweet potatoes), photos of rainbow-colored julienned vegetables pointing in multiple directions, so pristinely perfect I was convinced they were plastic until I saw a worker scooping some out for a customer, photos of silvery mackerel with hemispheres of jewel-like citrus woven through the fish fillets, photos of bento, photos of wagyu so marbled with fat, the color was almost entirely white. Photos, photos, photos. It wasn't until a young Japanese man approached me and asked seriously, in English, "Why are you taking photo?" that I realized that maybe it was impolite (illegal?) to do so. He said, in his halting English, "Can I ask you questions?"

I had already been thinking about Japanese prisons, the logical response when faced with a spotless and seemingly crime-free city like Tokyo. More than 37 million people in its metro area and during the week I was there I didn't see any trash, crime, or even anyone remotely creepy besides Matthew. I hadn't once been ogled or felt uncomfortable, a weekly occurrence back home. Perhaps, I hypothesized, Japanese prisons are like the Soviet Gulag for those who step out of line. The streets are so clean because if you litter you go to prison, get strung upside down, and are forced to eat all the shitty food that Japan produces strictly for criminals. Oh, and are forced to listen to all the crap pop music that Japan seems to love. But hey, Japan loves cameras. Surely I'm not being detained.

Or am I?

"Um, sorry," I said to the guy in English, "am I in trouble?"

"Trouble," he says, lingering on the word, letting it

roll around on his tongue. "Trouble," he says again. He motions for me to follow him.

"Why? What's going on?" I ask his back. He turns and says, "Yes, good, thank you."

I walk behind him and look at a huge display of pristine whole fish, the scales reflecting the light back into my unblinking eyes. I check my phone and see that there is one percent battery left. *Goodbye Matthew,* I think. *I wish you would have told me about the photo laws.*

We maneuver around a colorful, corner display of *tsukemono* (fermented vegetables). The man leads me up to three other people (department store security officers? local police?) and I see something sticking out of the woman's hand. Handcuffs? No, wait. It's a microphone. A microphone? Her English is a little better.

"Thank you for agreeing to do interview!"

"Sure," I say, the color returning to my face, "happy to do it!"

## MATTHEW

Becky, I hate you.

Look, I know how disappointed you were when it turned out that woman wasn't bearing handcuffs. But let's focus on me for a minute. I've been to Japan five times and have never been on a Japanese TV show.

I've certainly watched plenty of Japanese TV. My favorite show is First Errand, a series in which preschool kids are forced to run errands by themselves, unaware that a camera crew is following them. Hey, two-year-old! Walk across town in the rain and fetch me some tofu! Do you love watching kids cry? Then you'll love First Errand.

My other favorite show is Ultraman Dash. In this one, people have to carry out ordinary tasks under extraordinary conditions. A guy in a suit delivers a report to his boss's desk...on a BMX bike, without touching the floor. A waitress delivers an omelet...on water skis.

My third favorite show is Kōhaku Uta Gassen, a New Year's Eve men-vs-women singing contest, festooned with bubblegum melodies and confetti costumes.

I think I'd be great on any of these shows. I can totally walk across town and get some tofu, and I've even sort of learned how to use an umbrella. I watched a bunch of BMX bike movies when I was in middle school, so I'm probably great at that. And I'm pretty good at karaoke, as Becky never found out because she refuses to sing.

The kind of Japanese show I actually have a chance of being on is the kind where the host rounds up some foreigners and asks them what they're doing in Japan and what they think of it. Japanese viewers seem to have an unlimited appetite for this format. On the flight over, we watched a show about *izakaya* (Japanese pubs). A panel of foreigners, each embodying their national stereotypes (stylish Italian guy! American woman with out-of-control cleavage—not that I noticed!), went out to eat and drink at various izakaya. Then they came back to the studio to answer questions like, "Do you think people in your country would enjoy eating at a Japanese izakaya?"

I've heard many tales of visitors to Japan blundering into a TV show—sometimes even a regular spot on one—so I figured it had to happen to me sooner or later. So naturally it happened to Becky the first time she went out by herself.

"They kept asking me about the expensive melons and why I loved Japanese food," Becky reported. Ah, the expensive melons.

The Legend of the Expensive Melons came to America in the '80s. We studied Japan in my fourth grade class. We learned about sushi and textiles and ninjas. That's probably where I first heard that melons cost $100 in Japan. Like a lot of what you hear about Japan, it's sort of true.

I sent Becky to a depachika because, as she explained, it's the most absurdly concentrated and bewildering high-end food shopping experience in the world. Okay, I haven't been everywhere, and maybe there's some food hall in Dubai that's 147 stories tall and features a penthouse suite where you can slip the guard a $100,000 bill and go party like a boss with a bunch of $500 melons.

Back here in Japan, however, the depachika is where it's at. The best depachika, like Takashimaya, have well over a hundred stalls. It's less like a farmers market and more like the main floor of an American department store, with multiple perfume and luxury accessory counters, except here the perfume is fermented daikon and the luxury accessories are, well, melons.

A depachika is built for gawking. Becky and I visited one of my favorites, Isetan, together. Here's a stand selling assorted varieties of Spanish Iberico ham, hanging from hooks and sliced to order, $100 a pound, presumably to put on your Pizza Hut delivery. There's one selling a rainbow of sugared fruits. Or are they? "Ask him what that is," said Becky, pointing to a reddish slice gleaming with sugar crystals.

"I think it's a persimmon," I said smugly. "Hey, is that a persimmon?" I asked the guy behind the counter.

He shook his head. "It's carrot."

Well, close enough.

Visiting a depachika will teach you things about yourself that you didn't know. Apparently I'm really into salads. Or at least the glistening, perfectly composed sculptures of daikon matchsticks and sliced beets and plump shrimp and other delights. Becky and I gawked at the salad displays like we were encountering our first Playboy. They were so...intriguing! And oddly blemish-free! And glistening! We were too embarrassed to ask whether they were using some kind of salad lube. (By the way, and don't ask how I know this, the word for lube in Japanese is *rabu rōshon:* "love lotion.")

Aha! I've figured out what kind of Japanese TV show

I most want to star in. It would be a reality show based on that Tom Hanks movie about the guy who lives at the airport, only I'd live in a depachika, beg for leftovers, and date a suspiciously blemish-free ham saleslady. It could be called *The Underground Gourmet.* In every episode, the authorities would be about to catch me and throw me out of the store, but I'd steal a uniform and slip behind the nearest counter and blend right in.

"That, sir, is no persimmon," I'd say.

## BECKY ✿

By the way, the TV crew never followed up with me to let me know where I could view the show. Since I've never seen the footage, I'm left to believe it was a huge hit and now I'm a really big deal over there but they think I'm dead. Next time Matthew and I visit, swarms of hot girls will surround me, calling my name and holding up facsimiles of the melon I last touched. I will be Japan's Rodriguez. They've been searching for Sugar Woman, and now I'm here! They will ask Matthew to take photos with me. He will agree, bitterly.

# TEMPLE OF SOBA

## MATTHEW

People have a lot of weird phobias, okay? I won't make fun of your fear of balloon animals if you let me have my fear of making reservations.

This phobia has many levels.

I hate talking on the phone in general. In person I'm a decent conversationalist, but get me on the phone and I could be confused for an automated phone system. (I'm sorry, all of our operators are currently assisting other customers.) When my wife got a smartphone, it was like getting married all over again, because suddenly we could communicate remotely without it sounding like a dialogue from an English for Dummies CD. ("I am fine, spouse. How are you doing today?")

When the reservation time I want is unavailable, it feels like a personal rejection. Like, if I were George

Clooney or the creator of the Zagat Guide, I know I'd get that reservation. I know I'm not Clooney; you don't have to remind me.

I'm afraid they're going to ask me a question I'm not sure how to answer. Like, "Would you like to be seated in our Chef's Atelier?" I don't know, is the chef going to sit in my lap? Does the chef look like George Clooney?

Luckily, I've found two ways to live my life without having to face my fears: Avoid restaurants that require reservations, and make reservations online when I have to.

Before our trip, Becky and I talked about what kind of eating we wanted to accomplish in Tokyo. The city has almost 100,000 restaurants, so we probably weren't going to make it to more than half of them in a week. "How about a nice soba place?" I asked. I'd never been to one before, and I knew that soba was Tokyo's most refined and revered noodle, nut colored twirls of whole-grain satisfaction.

Works for me, said Becky.

So I went online to look for a fancy soba restaurant near our apartment. I came up with Soba Daian in Shinjuku. The reviews were good, the location was central, and best of all, they took reservations online. I told the website we wanted to eat on Saturday night at seven o'clock, and I hit send.

Then my heart sank when I realized I had requested a reservation for 07:00, otherwise known as 7 a.m. Not only was I going to have to call the restaurant, explain my blunder, and ask for a reservation at the proper time, but I'd have to do it in Japanese.

A cheerful reservationist answered the phone. "Uh, hello," I began. "I'm Matthew Amster-Burton, from America." This doesn't sound any less stilted in Japanese than it does in English.

I should clarify here for any worried readers that even though less English is spoken in Japan than in a lot of other countries you may have visited, a popular restaurant in a highly touristed neighborhood in Tokyo will definitely have an English speaker on hand to take calls from bewildered Americans. I'm just too stubborn to take advantage of the opportunity, so I pressed on. "I made a mistake with my reservation," I said. (Something delightful about Japanese is that "to make a mistake" is a simple transitive verb: *machigaeru.* So what I actually said was more like, "I mistaked the reservation." I guess we have a word like that in English, too: "blow.")

"Oh yes, we know who you are," said the woman on the phone. She fixed the reservation time. I started to thank her and hang up, but then came the hard questions. "How did you hear about the restaurant?"

"The internet."

"So what would you like to eat when you're here?"

"Uh, soba?" I replied. "Maybe sashimi?"

"Good," she said. I still have no idea why she asked this. Maybe they have a problem with people coming to the restaurant looking for sushi or something else they don't serve.

Shinjuku was just a five-minute train ride from our apartment in Takadanobaba, and we arrived early in case the restaurant was hard to find. It wasn't, so we walked through the streets to the east of Shinjuku station, among clothing stores, drinking establishments, and lots of other noodle restaurants. We stopped in at the original location of Kinokuniya, one of Japan's largest bookstore chains (they have a store in Seattle, too), to browse cookbooks and see if I could find my book. On a previous visit to Tokyo, I'd found it displayed prominently near the front of the store. Now that the book was six months old, it had been relegated to a shelf in the back corner of the basement level, in the "travel books you forgot about" section.

Well-deserved blows to my ego always make me hungry, so we headed to the restaurant. Pictures of high-end soba restaurants always make them look like the interior of a teahouse from a martial arts movie, where the hero goes to reflect before the final battle. Tatami rooms, *koto* music, hushed tones. Soba Daian has private rooms, but the main part of the restaurant isn't like that at all. It's lively, bustling, and centered around a big open kitchen. We sat at the bar in front of a glass window, behind which a chef was grilling meats and making salads. Becky and I immediately developed a chef-crush on this guy, whose plating skills were insane. With a few flicks of his chopsticks he could artfully arrange a platter of appetizers or a salad. I would need a week and a pair of tweezers to do what this guy did in seconds.

The waitress delivered our *otsumami* (amuse-bouche), two perfect gelatinous cubes of...well, what was it? I tasted, figured it out, and challenged Becky to do the same. This is probably the most insufferable game food people play with each other, although that's a long list. I won. "It's *gomadōfu,*" I explained: sesame tofu. It's not actually tofu at all, just sesame paste thickened with starch. It's also really, really good.

One of the pleasures of eating in another country is discovering the delicious common foods of that country that haven't made it to your own. Nowhere is this more true than Japan. It's like Japanese cuisine had to get past some immigration officials with fascistic tendencies on the way to America. Sushi, you can come in. Tempura, you're okay, but you have to be accompanied by another dish at all times. Sukiyaki got special dispensation during the '60s via a guest worker program. Ramen recently had its green card stamped.

So you grow up in America believing that people in Japan eat sushi, tempura, and ramen. And they do, along with hundreds of other dishes. One of these is *sobagaki,* which is not going to make it past the Commandant anytime soon.

Sobagaki are soba dumplings. Not a thin envelope of dough around a savory filling like Chinese dumplings. Sobagaki are like what you you find in a pot of American chicken and dumplings, made from flour (buckwheat flour, in this case), water, and nothing else. Stodgy, in other words. But what wonderful stodge: Sobagaki is earthy, smooth, and a little springy. It's excellent with soy sauce or in broth.

We enjoyed some crispy fried eel bones, chilled sake, and finally a wicker basket of soba. The noodles were thick and rustic, country-style, flecked with visible grains of buckwheat, served with a soy-based dipping sauce. Later, we found a window where you could peek into the soba master's chamber and watch him roll out the dough with a massive rolling pin and slice it by hand with a deadly-looking rectangular noodle knife. While the soba was delicious, we couldn't stop talking (and drooling, and moaning) about the daigaku imo from the appetizer plate.

## BECKY ✿

If I were a doctor of food, the first thing I'd do is whip out my prescription pad and write you an Rx for daigaku imo, also known as "university" or "college" potatoes. Essentially a fried and lacquered Japanese sweet potato, daigaku imo are purple on the outside, light yellow on the inside, with a sweet, crackly exterior and pillowy, carby-sweet interior. They are shiny, crunchy, and coated with toasted sesame seeds and are a nearly perfect food. Most recipes also call for a bit of soy sauce to balance the sweetness.

If you were in my office complaining of mild depression, I'd prescribe one cup. Constipated? Three cups. Nostalgic for your trip to Japan? Make five batches of it at home and don't share it with anyone. I'm not sure of this fact, but I feel fairly confident that the university students who have been eating this dish since the 1900s (see cheap + starch + hot + cheap) complain regularly of having trouble losing the Daigaku Imo Freshman 15.

Of course, I didn't know anything about this dish before I landed in Tokyo. As Matthew mentioned, many of the amazing dishes of Japan are truly foreign to most foreigners. His theory is that it is the work of fascist immigration officials on our side. My theory? It's the Japanese government keeping the good stuff to itself.

From my one-week trip to Tokyo, I can say with absolutely no authority that I think Japan is pretty darn special, the cleanest place I've traveled to and certainly one with the most vibrant, diverse, and consistently delicious cuisines. If too many people know about these great dishes, we will most definitely screw them up as only Americans can, diluting and weakening the originals to the point where tourists will ask for daigaku imo and really want yam nuggets dipped in ranch dressing, covered with powdered sugar. To wit: most Sicilians don't recognize half the food served at Italian-American "Sicilian" joints. Japanese bureaucrats held a closed-door meeting and they were all, "We're going to nip that bastardized bullshit version of *chawanmushi* or *oden* right in the bud." Except they said that in Japanese and filed it in triplicate. So, sorry to say, you're going to probably have to go to Japan to get this dish, or get comfortable making it yourself. (Easier said than done: I'm a professional, and my home attempts have fallen short. Might I suggest you go to Japan?)

Daigaku imo is incredible for a number of reasons, but most importantly because it finally erases the memory of that most blasphemous of Thanksgiving dishes, one that my dear grandmother specialized in—whipped sweet potatoes, topped with marshmallows and Red Dye No. 4 maraschino cherries. Or that equally cloying Southern U.S. dish of Candied Orange Diabetes whereby you take an already sweet, sweet potato and dump two cups of white sugar on it, plus perhaps maple syrup and honey and corn syrup, and serve it with meat and still feel justified calling it a vegetable.

Now, I'm no macrobiotic quinoa warrior, but I believe dessert belongs on the dessert cart and not on my dinner plate. When I mainline Nerds™ or Zours™ or Fun Dip™, I know I'm not eating a meal. It's more of an amuse-bouche.

At Soba Daian Restaurant, when I saw "assorted fall appetizers" on the menu I was hoping for anything chestnut, one of my favorite things in the world—warm, starchy, tender, nutty. Unless you're some sort of Japanese food nerd you will probably just be guessing at most of what's on the plate. What we got was a beautifully arranged set of little plates with roasted, peeled chestnut, skewered ginkgo nut, glazed mackerel, *kinpira gobō* (burdock, hijiki and carrot salad), lotus root that had its holes stuffed with mustard, and my new best friend daigaku imo. When you are in Tokyo, if you ever see these words on the menu: "assorted fall appetizers" (preferably in the actual fall), you must promise me you'll order it.

When we first sidled up to the counter, I promptly noted that my knees were crunching up against the bar, which left me with one of those long-legged "these places are not built for you people" split-decision moments to negotiate. Sit side-saddle away from Matthew and risk a catastrophic neck injury while conversing? Straddle the bar and rub one knee with Matthew and the other with whomever was on my left? Face Matthew and wrap my legs around him like he's one of those chicken wire false monkey mothers? Or (what I eventually went with) push back far enough so that your knees fit, but your ass is precariously perched off the end of the stool? Need added excitement with your meal? Sit like that.

It's truly hard to make a pig of oneself in a soba restaurant. Each dish is expertly plated, refined, restrained. Dishes are small and come out one by one. Pickles are offered to cleanse the palate. That's fine, but what I really wanted was a 50-piece bucket of daigaku imo.

# MOLTEN HOT SUGAR ROPE

## MATTHEW

As soon as Becky and I discussed the possibility of tempura for dinner, I thought of Tenta.

Tenta is a tiny little bar with about eight seats along a bustling street with dozens of other restaurants. It serves almost exclusively tempura. You order a beer and call out a few a la carte tempura pieces, and they'll be breaded and fried to order by a surprisingly unharried chef.

It's the Japanese equivalent of a Scottish chip shop that will fry anything, although they frown on patrons bringing in Black Thunder bars from the nearby Family Mart. The menu is at least fifty items long, and that's not including the tempura set meals and sashimi that I've never seen anyone order. The menu is nearly all vegetables and seafood, with an occasional hint of bacon.

But it's kind of a squirmy feeling when you take someone to one of your favorite restaurants, right? It's like the moment in a relationship when you discover that your significant other hasn't seen your favorite movie. As soon you curl up on the couch, you realize, hey, this isn't just a referendum on *Fast and Furious: Tokyo Drift,* it's a referendum on our relationship and on me as a human being. (Have you seen *Fast and Furious: Tokyo Drift?* If not, come over tonight. We can do hand stuff under the blanket, but not during the racing scenes.)

So it was kind of a relief when I went to Japan's most popular restaurant listing website (tabelog.com) and read that Tenta is closed Sundays. The referendum was off. I dug up another tempura place a few blocks away that looked fine. Becky and I hopped the Tozai Line to Nakano, my old neighborhood.

In a city of—no exaggeration—over a thousand neighborhoods, Nakano is my favorite. Not that I've visited them all. Not that I've visited even fifty. I just fell into the place. A couple years ago I was looking for a short-term apartment rental in Tokyo for my family, and found one in Nakano. It's a bit like the East Village of Tokyo: Low-rise but very urban, crammed full of good restaurants that go in and out of business constantly.

Because Nakano was my first real experience of Tokyo, I don't trust my opinion about it. I don't want to be like that guy who is really obsessed with a band's first album and is sure that they never improved on it. So I'll walk us through and then make Becky tell you what she thought of the place.

As we emerged from Nakano station, Becky pointed at the Sun Mall and said, "That looks cool."

"Great, that's where we're headed," I replied. The Sun Mall is like any number of glass-covered shopping arcades throughout Tokyo. This is an underappreciated urban form. There are almost no glassed-in arcades in Seattle, which is nuts, because I'm sure they're cheaper to build and maintain than a fully enclosed mall, and they combine some of the best features of being indoors and outdoors. The glass roof keeps out the rain, but the air tastes cleaner; natural light streams in during the day; your ears aren't assaulted by the echoey rancor of an indoor mall; and you can turn off onto an uncovered side street any time you like.

Which we did, squeezing into the alley between a *takoyaki* (savory octopus dumpling) stand and a bento deli, near the Copo sock store ("Copo: Here we have all kinds of socks"). We walked half a block past two ramen shops, a fugu restaurant, a coffee shop, two camera stores, an oyster shack, and a pachinko parlor, then paused in front of Life Supermarket, where I used to shop for groceries. "There's the parking lot," I said, indicating a corral jammed with two hundred bicycles.

"Like, for the whole neighborhood?" asked Becky.

"No, just the supermarket."

We turned and walked up the pedestrian street sometimes known as Nakano Ramen Street, although it also has plenty of seafood, hot pot, yakitori, and barbecue beef restaurants, plus bars and nightclubs. "And there," I began, "is the tempura place that's cl—wait, actually it's open."

Indeed, Tenta was open and bustling. Naturally! It's the kind of restaurant that opens when it feels like it, not according to a schedule on some website. Even though it was too early for dinner, I thought about dragging Becky inside, just in case they were planning to close at 6:30 p.m., which happened to me once before. (Admittedly, it was New Year's Eve.) But why play my crazy cards now?

We kept walking. We crossed Waseda-dōri and passed under the sign heralding the path to Arai Yakushi temple. Here the street was a little quieter and more temple-y in atmosphere, with antique shops and rice cracker stands. We stopped and peered into a candy store called Papabubble, then went inside to find a scene from *Moby Dick:* On first glance, the employees of Papabubble were wrestling sweatily with the red and engorged entrails of a sea monster.

❶ 注いで！*(POUR IT!)*

❷ こねて！*(KNEAD IT!)*

❸ 巻いて！*(ROLL IT!)*

❹ 伸ばして！*(STRETCH IT!)*

❺ 切って！*(CHOP IT!)*

❻ 壊して！*(DESTROY IT!)*

## BECKY ✿

I can't believe he passes it over to me on the heels of the phrase "red and engorged entrails of a sea monster." Not that it's an inaccurate metaphor. Indeed, the Papabubble guy was huffing and puffing, his ropey arm muscles rippling like hard candy ribbons as he pulled on the molten-hot sugar rope.

And no, Matthew, molten-hot sugar rope is not a euphemism.

But back to the whole red/engorged metaphor: It's accurate, yes; however, I don't like to see the crude words "engorged" and "monster" in reference to something so innocent and pure: namely my addiction to powdery white straight-from-the-cartel-grade sugar in the form of any candy, anywhere, anytime.

Papabubble originated in Barcelona and—fun fact—is pronounced "papa boo-blay" in both Spanish and Japanese. It's like Michael Bublé but even more sickeningly sweet. Part of the fun is the free show. As soon as Ropey Arms has stretched out the candy, he passes it off to a guy who cuts the rope into three-foot sections. Cutting Dude passes the candy over to Ice Girl who maintains the candies' shape and cools them by moving them back and forth under her gloved hands. When cool, the pieces of candy get chipped off with the edge of a large metal spatula into neat little discs and their happy ending arrives when they are scooped up, funneled into plastic bags, weighed, and sold. Freebies are plentiful and children (and shameless adult sugar addicts) line up for samples. The chain has taken off in Tokyo and there are shops in Amsterdam, Taipei and New York City, among other places. I can see why. When I was a kid, the most entertainment I got with my candy was watching my best friend Leslie Fanciulli puke up two pounds of barely-chewed Whoppers and Circus Peanuts.

Matthew and I hadn't eaten anything substantial yet, and while I thought I wasn't hungry when we first did the Tenta walk-by, it turns out that was prematurely-released stomach propaganda. I was suddenly ravenous. You know how when you're really hungry and rational decision-making becomes difficult? I told Matthew that we had to stay put so I could queue up for buckets of molten hard candy with cute little skulls or umbrellas or hearts inside.

So we hung out in the candy store watching the show, and I insisted to Matthew that I just had to wait for this particular batch of orange-scented candy to be finished so I could buy some as a gift. A gift for a special lady. Someone capable of eating it all furtively, later that evening, in a single-minded Orange Crush–flavored binge.

# LIVE NUDE EELS

## BECKY ✿

Full disclosure: I wrote a cookbook on sustainable seafood in 2011. This qualifies me to come to your town and be a preachy buzzkill at your favorite sushi bar. In Seattle I eat at Mashiko because Chef Sato has already vetted all the ingredients and we share similar ethics when it comes to all things fishy, environmental, and delicious. At Mashiko I turn off my internal menu analyzer and eat whatever he puts in front of me.

When you're a guest, on the other hand, it really behooves you to leave your opinions at the door. I act a bit differently when I meet someone at a place of their choosing or in their house. Unless it's my friend Henry and he orders the bluefin tuna and then I scream, "WHY ARE YOU RAPING THE OCEANS?" If it's anyone other than Henry, I will quietly pick some good choices for myself and refuse to offer complimentary evaluations of what's on other people's plates. If I'm in someone's home I eat whatever they offer me and say thank you sincerely.

Ordering food in a foreign language is just a whole other kettle of fish—frankly, I'm just happy when actual food arrives on my plate and not a matchbook and socks. On the practical side of things, I'm in Tokyo and I don't know how to say RAPING THE OCEANS in Japanese, and Matthew is graciously taking me to his favorite places, so I've put myself on a strict "don't ask, don't yell" policy for the short time I'm here. I will eat whatever deliciousness the place is serving, environmentalism be damned. And it's not like I killed the fish in any direct way; it's already dead.

Or is it?

When we walked into Tenta, the first thing I saw was a tank of live eels stage left. I realized immediately how long it's been since I've eaten one and oh my god, how good I remember them tasting. I will not tell you why it's been years since I've had eel (*unagi* specifically) because to do that and then tell you all about us eating them requires more sanctimonious hypocrisy than I am willing to admit to. Instead, I'm just going to drop the words "live eel" in here and move on.

There's getting close to your food and then there's eating eel at Tenta. When Matthew pointed to the tank, the sturdy chef leaned over the bar, his heft balanced ballet-like for such a thick-chested man as he plunged his meaty arm into the tank. He pulled out two wiggling eels, lifted them up and over the bar, and onto his cutting board, plunged a short metal spike into their heads, stripped the skin, and cut off the fillets in about 30 seconds. He then tied the skeletons into two perfect knots and had everything battered and into the fryer before Matthew and I had time to clean up from the tidal wave of water that had doused our necks.

As my teeth broke through the shattering salty spine, I had this thought: If, because of this meal, we are implicated in eating the *last remaining inhabitants of the ocean*, at least eat all the parts. Was this the best tempura I'd ever had? It was crispy, crunchy, and fresh, served with an ice cold beer in a foreign country with a free show. So, yes.

The remaining eels eventually calmed down and went back to contemplating whatever it is that eels choose to think about.

"Do you think they realize two of their buddies just bit it?" I asked Matthew, and he pondered that meaningfully as he popped a crispy chunk of eel skeleton into his mouth.

"I mean, do you think," I continued, "do you think they're in there like 'John! John! John! John!'"

"Oh my god, Frank? FRANK!"

MMM...
WHITE MEAT.

# BAD STUDENTS

## BECKY ✿

When Matthew asked me if I was interested in taking a cooking class with Nagomi Visit, a nonprofit that offers classes in Japanese cuisine in locals' homes, there was really only one appropriate, if not ignorant, question: Will I fit through the door of a Japanese person's home? At nearly six feet tall, I had already struggled with robe sizing, bar stool leg room, and navigating bathrooms built for mini-me, not actual me. I was so focused on imagining myself ducking into a hobbit hole, that when we stepped into teacher Yuko Omiya's home, it took a second to register her tall Venezuelan husband, Akio.

By this point in the trip, the whole take your shoes off at the door thing was old hat, so when Yuko gently and kindly taught us that you are actually supposed to take your shoes off and step up one by one onto the step without touching your sock to the contaminated shoe area, I could only glare back at Matthew as if it was his fault I was now carrying Hepatitis C and Ebola into our lovely host's home. (Well, the Nagomi Visit website did say it was customary to bring a gift.) It's funny how the common sense of this particular form of etiquette blew right by both of us despite the fact that neither of us wear shoes into our homes back in Seattle. Little did we know that we were simply transferring germs around our house in our socks. 'Merica! Let's take Japanese tradition and totally screw it up!

It was only months later, back in Seattle, that I found this little gem on the Nagomi Visit blog under the heading "How to be an Amazing Nagomi Guest":

> Practice the art of taking off your shoes. You may already take off your shoes at the front door in your own home but give the Japanese-way a try.

The idea is: don't take off your shoes and then encrust your socks with filth by placing them on the floor in the entrance area. Instead, slip your feet out of your shoes and immediately step up and out of the lowered entrance area and into the house with balletic grace, possibly also putting on slippers as part of the same maneuver. "Don't worry too much about these sorts of details," the website continues, "as you are hopefully going to become good friends with your host."

In other words, don't worry, we know you're going to fuck this up. Hello, Yuko and Akio! Thank you for offering up your home to teach us about Japanese cuisine.

Might we offer you this gift from our home in return? You'll find it all over your floor. To really appreciate our generosity, use a black light.

But really, we were here to learn, cook, and eat, so enough about Matthew's contaminated socks. On the menu there were three dishes, two of which I was familiar with: *chirashizushi* ("scattered sushi") and *karaage* chicken (small nuggets of fried chicken) and one that was new to me (and now on a monthly winter rotation at home): *tonjiru* (pork and miso stew). Yuko was kind and hospitable. She has a passion for cooking combined with a certain tenacity and strength women chefs tend to have. Yuko, like myself, spent many years in the restaurant business (a mostly man's world), working her way up before going out on her own to teach cooking classes, among other culinary pursuits. She was a badass and I instantly liked her.

The cooking instruction was stellar, the food fantastic, getting to hang out with Yuko and Akio and talk food and Japan: sincerely awesome. Seeing Matthew wear a slightly emasculating bib apron? Priceless.

## MATTHEW

What Becky doesn't understand is that I love wearing aprons. Every night I sit down to dinner wearing a long, black apron, and you know why? Because it keeps the food off my pants. Given that food and clothing get along so poorly, it's really odd that we're constantly putting them in close proximity. Japan doesn't have any answer to this, although a few ramen shops offer bibs.

Because I'm a problem-solver, I'd like to propose two potential solutions.

**Jumpsuits.** You know how some fancy restaurants offer men a dinner jacket if they're uncouth enough to show up without one? Let's expand this idea to all restaurants, but make it a slimming, machine-washable black jumpsuit that looks great on everybody and de-emphasizes stains. This started out as a joke but now I really, really want this to happen. Or if it can't...

**Nudity.**

As for tracking dirt into the house, the thing I want to know is: Why do we need etiquette when we have technology? If there's one thing Becky and I learned in Japan, it's that the salve for the sting of daily existence is a high-tech toilet. So why don't we have electronic foot-sterilizing pads? Sure, a power surge would inevitably singe someone's foot off, but it's totally worth the risk.

So when we got back from Japan, I tried to learn to step in and out of my shoes with silent grace. Every time I ended up flinging a shoe against the wall or squishing the back of the shoe with my heel. Isn't that the worst feeling? In my own personal Hell, I'm going to be forced to walk around that way.

Oh, wait, we went to a cooking class, right? Well, it was just as great as Becky says, and she didn't even mention that Yuko taught us to make *tamagoyaki* (a rolled omelet) just because Becky said she was interested in learning how.

I suspect we were each a different type of bad student. Becky was the person whose skills are too good for the class, like the kid who shows up to Spanish 101 after spending the summer in Mexico. I was the know-it-all who couldn't chop an onion but would ask questions like, "Do you think the best kombu comes from Hokkaido?"

One of my favorite things about visiting Yuko and Aiko happened before we even got to their house. Becky and I were running early, because I'm neurotic about being on time. This is a popular trait in Tokyo, which is a very punctual society, although getting to our destination 45 minutes early was probably unnecessary.

However, it gave us an opportunity to scope out the neighborhood, buy some candy at the train station, and stop off at a chain café. Becky and I both ordered soy milk matcha lattes. This is something I would never drink in America, not just because I'm a snob but because it would be overly sweetened and made with terrible soy milk. Here, it was delicious, with waves of fresh soy and green tea flavor, and not too sweet. This was out in a random suburb whose name I don't even remember. If we'd been in the U.S. we would have ended up at a gas station snacking on Flamin' Hot Funyuns washed down with burnt coffee, the air perfumed with a cocktail of petroleum distillates—which actually sounds pretty good, but probably just because I'm thinking about the *Fast and Furious* series again.

# SHOPPING HEAVEN, SHOPPING HELL

## BECKY ✿

You know when you've heard and read about something forever and when you finally go there yourself, it's kind of anticlimactic? Yeah, that totally didn't happen at Tsukiji.

Tsukiji (pronounced Skee-ji) is the largest fish market in the world and a complete sensory assault. It was simultaneously everything I imagined and nothing I imagined. My friend Luuvu—recently of Seattle, now of Tokyo—was my guide. Several of his friends met us at the train station and jumped in on the tour. A cold, sideways rain was slapping us in the faces as we huddled under our umbrellas and headed on foot straight into the heart of the market, a cavernous warehouse of a million aisles where the business of selling fish goes on, much of it wholesale, and a great deal of the fish live or just recently departed. When navigating through the inner bowels of the market, you are pulled and pushed past a veritable global aquarium. A chef with ADHD would need to walk through 9,000 times just to focus on maybe a third of the 450 reputed species being sold here. Greenpeace be damned, everything in the oceans has a price at Tsukiji (whale meat, anyone?).

We got a quick look at the open area in the inner market where the famed bluefin tuna auction had taken place at some ungodly hour that morning. The outer market houses various knife and kitchen shops, tamagoyaki joints, ramen shops, and more, including the famous sushi restaurants where patrons line up for hours waiting for divine slabs of sashimi and nigiri sushi. We did not line up for sushi. In fact, we never went out for sushi the entire week we were in Tokyo.

I will pause here for your shock and disgust.

You are not the only one to wonder why the hell not. It was the number one question I was asked after I told people I had been to the market: "So," they nearly squealed, "how did you like the sushi at Tsukiji?" Luckily I had a defense prepared. Here in Seattle, we are surrounded by fantastic sushi bars. One of Jiro Ono's former chefs lives in Seattle. Jiro, as in the documentary Jiro Dreams of Sushi (also as in the revered sushi chef who operates out of the Ginza train station). Seattle's "Jiro" is Shiro Kashiba, and he opened his own sushi bar here, Shiro's, in 1994. He just recently came out of semi-retirement to open a new place, called Kashiba. Lines form early to get a coveted seat at his bar. I'd add to my list some other incredible sushi chefs in my home town: Hajime Sato at Mashiko and Taichi Kitamura at Sushi Kappo Tamura. Simply put, we get really good sushi in Seattle. While in Tokyo for such a short trip, I wanted to eat things I had never had before and things that we don't (yet) do that well back home, like *tsukemen* (a form of ramen where the eater dips fat wheat noodles into a rich broth), okonomiyaki, and tempura, and while we are starting to get some fairly good ramen in the Seattle area, you don't really know that until you first eat ramen where ramen started. I suppose the same logic could apply to sushi in Japan but honestly, I also wasn't up to the expense, nor the long wait time. Incredible, inexpensive food with no wait times is the norm, not the exception in Tokyo. I can wait in a two-hour line on some other trip, to some other country; some other country that doesn't have a 99 percent deliciousness success rate.

But back to the inner market: I had read about the aggressiveness of the small truck operators at Tsukiji and assumed it was exaggerated, especially after a week of Japanese-style street courtesy, but I was wrong. It's not so much that they want to kill you; it's more that they are doing their job very fast and their job has nothing to do with keeping you alive.

A few aisles past what must be the world's most impressive display of fish so long and skinny they didn't even fit in their boxes, I found oodles of tiny clams used for their briny broth in miso soup and mid-gawk I was shoved to the side with a firm hand and a sharp grunt. I was surprised and delighted to see that it was from a four-foot-something 60-year-old female fishmonger who had no patience for my seafood rubber-necking.

If Tsukiji were Pac-Man, I was getting eaten by the tiny turret trucks named Blinky, Pinky, Inky, and Clyde. Power pellets would naturally be little bites of sushi and well, I just told you I didn't eat any. I was losing Tsukiji Pac-Man but WINNING IN LIFE, because just over my shoulder there were endless boxes of live *amaebi* (sweet shrimp) and *this* girl was going to buy a kilo and gather my companions, twist their heads off (the amaebi, not my companions), and peel and eat them raw, still quivering with life, right there in the market. One of the Japanese wholesalers looked over at me as I ate, nodded his head and made a mysterious guttural sound which I interpreted as deep respect for my market choice, but it was probably just gas.

The shrimp stirred our hunger and between the rain, cold, and constantly being in everyone's way, we retreated to the outer market in search of a hot bowl of ramen. To describe where we ate lunch as a ramen restaurant is to really expand the concept of the word "restaurant." At Chuka Soba Inoue, this is what we were looking at: Two guys in a 100-square-foot kitchen, tops, one of them around 70 years old (the Master), tall, but bent over at the upper back with the repetitive work of pivoting from his huge pot of what tasted to me like a pork and chicken broth to the 10 plastic bowls lined up on the narrow counter bar. The other guy (the Apprentice), younger, but still not young, was in charge of replenishing product, doing dishes, and laying down the pork, *negi* (Japanese green onions) and *menma* (bamboo shoots).

It was a beautiful sort of ballet between these two men, with the Master taking the first dance. Into the bowls, he ladled *tare* (a seasoning base made with reduced soy sauce), threw in a handful of negi, and sprinkled some mystery powder (MSG? dashi powder? salt? all of the above?). He topped this off with a large ladleful of broth. Then the Master was back to a smaller pot, teasing hanks of ramen out of the water with long chopsticks in his right hand and nestling them up against a flat-sieved, long-handled tool in his left, systematically shaking the excess water out of the noodles with a distinct slup-slup sound of noodle meeting sieve. Then, he used the chopsticks to pile the noodles up in the middle of each bowl. As soon as the ramen hit the broth, the Apprentice took over, adding a generous portion of four pieces of pork loin on top (the pork was lean with just a thin edging of fat), more negi, daikon sprouts, and menma.

A woman, tough as nails and about as short as one, demanded our order. "Four," I blurted a nanosecond too slowly, fumbling for the correct change. She took our cash and led us firmly through the crushing crowd to a tall table, bussed it, cleaned it, and pushed us toward the empty spot. Not a seat, a spot, where you were to stand and slurp. I've never before been so happy to be shoved towards a slurping station.

Allow me to show you to your spot. In front of you: napkins, chopsticks, spoons, chili paste and raw garlic. To your rear, a cacophonous throng of people streaming past. You can feel them brush your back, but you barely notice—you're standing at the slurping station, bent slightly at the upper back, inhaling the porky, chickeny, umami-laden smell of heaven, holding up the noodles with your chopsticks to admire and appreciate them.

Everything goes quiet.

## MATTHEW

Silently communing with a bowl of noodles, huh? Must be nice. Meanwhile, I was exploring a place we've all heard of but few of us, other than Dante, have ever had the opportunity to see firsthand. Like the author of one of those dumbass books about visiting heaven, I have answers!

*Where is the entrance to Hell located?*
About 20 miles east of Tokyo. Actually, it has many entrances, including through the Toys R Us.

*Does Hell really have nine levels?*
Only three, but it features over 350 shops and restaurants and a floor area of over 4 million square feet.

*Does Hell ever freeze over?*
No, but there's a Cold Stone Creamery.

*Is Hell known by any other names?*
Many! The Underworld. Hades. Sheol. AEON Mall Makuhari New City.

*Does Hell have parking?*
Tons, but you'll never get a space on the weekend.

*So, to clarify, you're just complaining about going to the mall?*
Absolutely. Like any self-respecting urban dude, I love real city streets and find malls to be the exact opposite: sanitized, climate-controlled, wrung clean of any spark of life.

*But you're not just an obnoxious city guy, you're also a tedious Japanophile, and this mall was in Japan. Doesn't that make it inherently fascinating?*
No.

*How's the food in Hell?*
Not bad at all. You see, while Becky was getting all funked up with fish guts at Tsukiji, I visited friends in Chiba prefecture, in the eastern suburbs of Tokyo. In William Gibson's Neuromancer, Chiba is portrayed as a dystopian corporate technocracy. In reality, it's a lot like suburban Seattle—that is, a dystopian corporate technocracy.

AEON Mall Makuhari New City is the largest mall in Japan. It opened in fall of 2013. It's actually four malls (including a Pet Mall) fused together into a Frankenmall that any day now will become sentient and devour the juicy, delicious patrons (and pets) inside. My friends took me there because they have a baby daughter, and when you live in the suburbs and have a baby, you go to the mall on the weekend. This is true whether you live in Chiba, Cincinnati, or Cannes.

At Makuhari New City, you can shop for clothes at Hurly Burly Party, Algy, Hysteric Mini, or Lovetoxic. I bought my daughter Iris a pencil case decorated with Jiji the cat from the movie *Kiki's Delivery Service.* I held the baby and thought about lunch.

The word "hangry" was coined to describe me. If it's 1 p.m. and I haven't had lunch yet, I turn into the carnivorous plant from *Little Shop of Horrors.* (Despite what you may have read elsewhere in this book, this is my only flaw.) At the same time, I'm cognizant that the rules of society don't allow an adult person to burst into tears, yell "FEED ME!" and start biting people. As for those people who are able to drift through the day, eat when they feel like it, and skip a meal when it's convenient: those aren't people, they're killer robots wearing skin suits.

Finally we navigated to one of Makuhari New City's several food courts and looked for the place with the shortest line, which turned out to be a Miyazaki chicken restaurant called Miyazaki Nichinan Tsukada Farm.

Miyazaki is a region in southern Japan known for heritage free-range chicken, and Tsukada Farm serves it many ways, mostly char-grilled at lunch and hot pot–style at dinner. In Japan, char-grilled chicken (*sumibiyaki*) is a separate style from yakitori. Yakitori is grilled and served on skewers over very hot, clean charcoal, emphasizing the flavors of the chicken itself. Char-grilled chicken is cooked on a grate and served in chunks, having taken on an ashen layer of char. It looks like a pile of fireplace sweepings but tastes much better.

For lunch I ordered *oyakodon.* "Oyako" means "parent and child," and it's the vaguely grisly name for chicken (parent) and egg (okay, you get it) on rice. Normally oyakodon is made with chunks of chicken simmered in broth, but here it was made with char-grilled chicken. The smokiness of the chicken and rich, deep orange egg seeped into the rice along with the flavors of soy sauce, mirin, and dashi. I ate it, as is the custom, with a spoon.

Tsukada Farm is incomprehensible by American standards, and I still don't understand how it works or, really, how anything about food in Japan words. See, the thing is, Tsukada Farm is a big national chain. The chicken they serve is premium *jidori,* which refers to the breed, the humane, free-range protocol for raising it, and the promise to rush the birds to the restaurant promptly after slaughter. You can get jidori chicken in Seattle, but it's only served at a few high-end restaurants and is priced accordingly. The oyakodon at Tsukada is under $10. If you like to eat and you're not in Japan, what are you doing with your life?

So maybe AEON Makuhari New City isn't actually Hell. Maybe that distinction still belongs to the Mall of America.

# DRINKING PROBLEMS

## BECKY ✿

I don't have many regrets in life, but I really regret ordering a Blanton's bourbon at Ishinohana, a high-end cocktail bar in Shibuya. After all, it was a Japanese whisky—The Yamazaki Single Malt Whisky, Sherry Cask 2013—that won the 2015 World Whisky of the Year in *Jim Murray's Whisky Bible,* beating out Scottish distilleries for the first time and boosting the profile of Japanese whisky overnight. Scotch is an entirely different, and many would argue, more refined beverage than down-home, throat-burning, sweet-on-the-finish bourbon, but sometimes you just want what you want. And sometimes, when in Rome or Japan, you can be an idiot.

I love bourbon and Blanton's in particular, but I can drink that every day at home. Ishinohana is known for its seasonal cocktails infused with a long list of tempting ingredients: *yuzu* (a tart Japanese citrus fruit), kumquat, persimmon, cassis, in addition to the line-up of whiskies I spotted front and center. I wouldn't eat french fries and ketchup in Tokyo, so why am I drinking Kentucky bourbon here? This is just the kind of probing and profound question I will take to the grave, unanswered.

But were I to ponder an answer I'd say: I think I was intimidated.

I was also cocky. This entire trip I've been happily deferring to Matthew's knowledge and expertise in all things Tokyo, but when it comes to booze and bar culture, I know more than him. In other words, I have a drinking problem and he doesn't.

I could tell the minute I walked into this place that it was a temple for the serious and refined connoisseur of liquid courage. We stepped up to the bar and sat in front of the dapper bartender, nattily dressed in vest and tie. As I looked across at the sparkling bottles arranged perfectly on the shelves I saw Japanese whisky after Japanese whisky and I felt self-conscious about pointing at bottles and mumbling something indecipherable in my terrible Japanglish. My eyes fell on an old familiar friend and before I could think I blurted: "Blanton's!" I wanted to seem cool. So cool I would order the wrong thing in the wrong place in the wrong country. Matthew ordered some hand-crafted, house-squeezed yuzu cocktail shaken with ice from glacial runoff from an 85-million-foot peak. Matthew's drink was really really good. Matthew is such a dick.

If I lived in Tokyo I would be a regular at this bar for three reasons:

1. The artistry of the crystal clear, spherical, hand-carved ice cubes nearly made me stick its remains in my pants so I could smuggle it out. An engineer has to be on the payroll because when the bartender dropped it into the glass it touched both sides, a near perfect fit with just enough room for the booze to get around it.

2. The elegant efficiency of the bartender's movements were mesmerizing. Not nearly as showy or egomaniacal as craft mixologists in the States—there were no flames, no spinning glasses—but the precision of his movements, his hands moving so fluidly, so efficiently, so everywhere, half-man, half-octopus.

3. The glassware itself. It's not something you really think about until you get served a nice shot of bourbon over an ice cube in a crystal rocks glass. It's really, really hard to take a shot off a toilet seat lid after that.

I lied about only having one regret. I have another one. I wish I had ordered some food, because the English-language menu offered options like the Stick Salad. I'm sure it is a julienned salad of one thing or another, but why think about what it really is when you can be thinking about a bowl of sticks with vinaigrette. Interested in some offensive meat? Try, if you dare, the Prosciutto Crude from Italy. Or simply a little peckish? Take a gander at the Nuts menu and perhaps you'll be tempted by "Giant Corn," which I'm assuming is a bowl of corn nuts but I really want it to be a four-foot cob of corn.

I swirled the last bit of bourbon around the glass and carefully tilted it towards my mouth stopping the 10-pound ice ball, just in time, before it could break my nose.

"Another?" the bartender's eyes asked me.

"Blahhnnton's" I slur and then drop my eyes in shame.

God damn it.

## MATTHEW

Then we got kicked out of the bar.

Well, not right away. But still.

After my fruity yuzu drink, I ordered an Old Fashioned. Becky is not kidding about the ice cube. It's literally a hand-carved sphere of ice, two inches in diameter, that nestles perfectly in a rocks glass.

The bartender didn't carve it in front of us, but you can watch the process on YouTube (search for "ice ball carving"). It's done with a chef's knife, and glistening shards fly everywhere as the bartender hacks away. If this operation were being performed in front of me, I'd sit with my mouth open to catch the crystal shrapnel on my tongue.

The cocktail was excellent, and once I finished it, I tried to figure out how to pull off my usual habit of slurping the ice cube into my mouth and clicking it around obnoxiously. Eventually I conceded that I was not going to be able to deep-throat this thing, and settled for caressing it idly with my finger.

When Becky says I don't have a drinking problem, she just means I have a different kind of drinking problem. My problem is, I'd love to be a social drinker, but my limit is one-and-a-half drinks, after which I get giggly, then overshare, then get sleepy. (I realize I've just described the entire point of drinking.) Then I have weird dreams and wake up the next day with my head feeling like a hand-carved ice ball, mid-carving process. After about three days of vacationing with Becky, I emailed my wife to complain that I couldn't keep up with Becky in the nightlife department. This lifestyle consisted of going out for one or two drinks and sometimes staying out past 11 p.m.

After I'd finished my second drink and gotten to third base with the ice ball, we paid the check, then sat around talking like idiots for another fifteen minutes. We'd forgotten, or were too sloshed to remember, that in Japan (like many countries) when you ask for the bill in a restaurant, it means you're ready to pay up and leave. We were committing a faux pas so egregious that the bartender asked us very politely if we would please make our seats available for the next party.

That's the long version. The headline is that Becky and I drank too much and got kicked out of a bar in Shibuya. The couple who'd been waiting patiently in the foyer were glad to take over our bar stools. Perhaps they were planning to order something exotic and imported. Something like Blanton's.

# TECHNICOLOR BUZZ

## MATTHEW

"You pick a place," I told Becky. We were walking down a street about five feet wide, lined on both sides with bars. Not, like, prison bars. Drinking establishments. Rock- and roll-themed bars. Country and western bars. Rowdy bars and empty dives. Bars called Private Tutor, Buoy, and Midnight + 1. (Wouldn't "Hey, Buoy" be a great name for a sailor-themed gay bar?) Many of the bars are themed: you go to talk photography, or motorcycles, or classic R&B records.

This is Shinjuku Golden Gai. It's six alleys crammed into an area of about two city blocks, with over 200 bars. The largest have maybe a dozen seats; the smallest, four or five. Some are off-limits to foreigners, some post English menus, and most fall somewhere in-between. Don't behave like a jerk or force the bartender to speak too much English, and you can hang out as long as you like.

I'd strolled through Golden Gai before but never stopped for a drink. We've already determined that I'm not much of a drinker, and I also never know what to order. (I mean, I know *now.* Blanton's.)

Also, I'm the kind of person who will spend an hour in the paper towel aisle asking myself, *Brawny or Bounty?* Mostly I admire Golden Gai for the urban design. It's a throwback to when Tokyo was as densely populated as a box full of packing peanuts. (Today's Tokyo is only as dense as a Chuck E. Cheese ball pit.) Golden Gai is sparkling, car-free, and surprisingly pleasant for an open-air drunk tank.

And it's under constant threat of redevelopment. Japan is long past the bubble years of the 1980s, when some parcels of land were on the market for $20,000 per square foot, but real estate is real estate, and Shinjuku is highly desirable. The hotel from *Lost in Translation* is here, along with the world's busiest train station. You can literally walk miles from one part of Shinjuku to another via the station's underground corridors, passing beneath neon karaoke palaces, nine-story camera shops, department stores, and restaurants. Walking through the tunnels is oddly like passing through the circulatory system of a massive underground creature, perhaps the sarlacc from Return of the Jedi. You start out in a slim, unadorned capillary, pass into a larger tunnel lined with noodle and plate lunch shops, and shoeshine stands (Mr. Minute is a popular chain, and also my nickname), and then through the heart of the station itself. When you can make it through Shinjuku without getting lost in a department store that you don't remember entering, that's a sign that you've put in your 10,000 hours in Tokyo.

Golden Gai is just a block from one of the Shinjuku station's hundred exits. Becky selected a bar seemingly at random. Later she explained that she was drawn in by the cute pigtailed bartender and the colorful ceramic tile decor. Becky ordered a bourbon while I had a long Brawny vs. Bounty moment with the menu and eventually alighted on the avant-garde choice of a gin and tonic.

The bartender, Minami, served our drinks, smoked a cigarette with Becky, and asked us where we were from and what we were doing in Japan. Becky managed to get into a conversation about bitters, while I frantically looked up the Japanese word for "bitters" on my phone. The answer: *bitaazu.* You're welcome. Minami lamented that customers at her place don't order the kind of serious cocktails made with bitters. I looked at my G&T and said nothing. She asked us if we'd heard of her favorite electronic music artist. Guess what: we hadn't!

We couldn't stay long at Minami's nameless bar, because we had to get to our next appointment, which Becky will tell you about. On the way, we saw two toughs throw a guy out of a bar and onto the pavement, exactly like in a movie. If I keep hanging out with Becky and drinking G&Ts, that's going to be me.

"Don't look it up," Matthew told me, "no really, don't Google it." All he would tell me was that he was taking me to a Robot Restaurant and he wanted it to be a surprise. Fine. I didn't need a search engine to tell me what seemed pretty obvious. I mean, it's Tokyo after all—a city where cats and owls have their own cafés and you can share lattes with them and you know, hang. A city where there are ninja restaurants, prison-themed eateries and vampire cafés, or so I've read. Until, of course, you ask a local and they say "yeah, I've never been there" and you realize that making generalizations based on the outer edge of a city's fringe culture is a little naive. I mean, imagine if people thought everyone in Seattle was obsessed with dressing up in mascot uniforms just because of that one article in that local rag a few years back. Just because we may have read about Furrics (and their conventions) doesn't mean we dress up as Squatch the SuperSonic and get it on with Jazz the Bear. At least not every day.

I tried not to form any preconceived ideas about what a Robot Restaurant would be beyond the obvious: I will eat life-altering sushi off of the hard metallic backside of a droid dressed in a slinky outfit. Because, duh, Robot Restaurant.

We arrived and descended a seemingly endless staircase into the depths of what seemed like a tutti-frutti, cotton candy-themed manga hell spiral. I got a little anxious: Is that an emergency exit or just a cartoon drawing of one?

It turns out that the Robot Restaurant is really not much of a restaurant. Imagine ballpark concessions at an automated drag queen revue and you're not too far off. I'd call the performance campy, but that implies more of a human touch and there were simply too many circuit boards to make the adjective work. Imagine if Liberace, a 10-foot Totoro, and Tron were sharing the stage with a very peppy, scantily-clad but totally PG cheerleader squad and drumline. Imagine still that the scene is loud, with taiko drums rattling the ribs in your chest, and slightly seizure-inducing, with the visual assault of a speed metal laser show. When I looked over at Matthew, his pupils were dilated, but I chalk that up to his one-drink binge.

We didn't eat at the Robot Restaurant. Our appetites were suppressed by the balls-to-the-wall sensory overload, which we could have predicted by this bit of text on the English version of their website: "The show also includes the use of bright flashing lights which may result in feeling ill in some cases." The Robot Restaurant is potentially fun for the whole family, though the website also mentions that the loud sounds might be uncomfortable for small children. (Or anyone with functioning ears, they might add.)

I realize I sound a bit *bitaazu* about the Robot Restaurant; I don't mean to. Sure I was a little disappointed when the cute girls only high fived me at the end of the show. But what most bothered me is that I lost out on an opportunity: getting it on with a sexy robot is a marriage loophole that I'm sure my wife would have totally supported.

# BEING AND NOTHINGNESS

## BECKY ✿

Five days in Tokyo and I'm not sure what I will miss most when I get home—the incredible food or the warm comfort of the toilet seats. I'll admit that I was one of those people who previously poo-pooed stories about those seats. "Oh my god," gushed every single friend who'd been to Japan, "those crazy warm seats—they're awesome." I'd only had one previous experience with them, at Mashiko, my favorite sushi bar in Seattle. I wasn't expecting the warmth and when I sat down I immediately whipped around to see whose lap I had sat on. It was disconcerting, to say the least. What I hadn't imagined is that I began to crave the experience in a way that is probably mildly dysfunctional.

I caught a cold in Japan, and the wind and rains conspired to keep me in our rental apartment a little too often until Matthew dragged me out of it. "It's your last full day in Tokyo!" he pleaded. We bundled up, grabbed our simple-but-brilliant translucent umbrellas (to better see the jostling wave of umbrellas coming at your head) and headed for a tea shop that he had been to the previous morning.

Next to warm toilet seats, there is little better than coming out of the driving cold rain on a busy neon-addled street to tuck into a tiny, cozy tea house, bathed in warm, low light reflecting off the dark wood ceiling. The decor was minimalist; the host was an elegant older woman, pleasantly and predictably hospitable. We ordered tea. It was green. It tasted good. Matthew will have a lot more to add to this. I will say that the accoutrements that came along with the tea were fascinating to a Japanese tea virgin. The little stone tea pot, with its long anteater proboscis coming out one end and its other more modest one on the other side—sure, it could have been for pouring tea but it could have been a nose flute or a neti pot.

I sat on my hands, afraid of all the entirely inappropriate things I might do with that pot.

I was here for the tea and comfort, yes, but I was also here to sample the mysterious dessert known as *cream anmitsu.* Matthew took one bite and quickly slid the dessert over to me, which didn't bode well. The guy loves sweets. It was a beautiful thing to look at, with translucent white and slightly opaque green cubes at the bottom, topped with two perfectly spherical white mochi dumplings, a shaggy mound of sweet azuki paste, and one deep green scoop of matcha ice cream, served with a small pitcher of sweetened matcha syrup to pour over the whole affair.

I started first with the azuki paste because beans never knew how good they were until they met this much sugar. The ice cold syrup and ice cream felt good on my throat. The mochi balls were the chewiest thing I've ever had in my mouth, and that's saying something. Because of my limited ability to breathe normally, I worried for just a second that the density and extreme taffiness of the balls would obscure my airway if I sniffled. I chewed them with the focus and urgency of someone worried for their life.

And then there were the agar-set cubes on the bottom of the bowl. They tasted more like nothing than nothing. They tasted so much like nothing that they pulled flavor out of my body from my previous meal. All I was given to focus on was the texture, which was perhaps the point. And yet, the texture seemed disturbingly like chewing on packing peanuts. No, not that... like candle wax, but less dense. Nope, not that either. Like eating the waterproofing caulk that seals your tub. Yes, remember how chewy that was? Just like that.

Irrationally, I kept going back to it. The complete absence of taste was fascinating. Perhaps you were meant to eat a little bit of the caulk along with a bit of the ice cream or syrup, but I had eaten everything else so just had a big pile of this stuff to crumble through. I ate it all. Why? Because it was like a palate brain-teaser. Fascinating stuff. I never really need to eat it again.

I excused myself to go to the bathroom, sat down onto my new best friend Toto, and nearly shot straight up into the pretty wood ceiling.

Lucky me. I found the only cold toilet seat in Tokyo.

## MATTHEW

See, I knew there was a reason I brought Becky to Tokyo: to eat all the cream anmitsu.

I'd first been to Chachakōbō tea house the day before, for a business meeting. "Why don't you pick a place to meet?" my colleague had suggested. I'd never met the guy in person before, so this sent me into a panic. It was like choosing a blind date venue. If I pick a chain place, will he think I'm boring? Does he like tea? Should I wear my good underwear?

Fortunately, I got lucky. With the tea place, I mean.

The next day, I roused Becky from her apparent deathbed and said something jerky like, "You're in the best city in the world, and you're NOT going to spend the whole day in bed." Fortunately for my testicles, she was too weak to fight back.

We walked past Takadanobaba station and the adjacent Big Box department store (Becky thought the name Big Box was really funny, for reasons I can't begin to fathom). We continued along Waseda-dōri for about half a mile, past ten-story karaoke dens and drugstores, soba restaurants and chain croissant bakeries. It was dim and rainy, the sky verging on *makkura,* the evocative Japanese adjective for "dark as shit." We shivered under umbrellas, walking single-file to avoid smashing into oncoming pedestrians. so I couldn't even check Becky's facial expression, but I assume she was thinking, "I can't believe I let this fucknut convince me to walk a mile in the rain."

I'm kind of an umbrella virgin. The only time I ever use an umbrella is in Japan, because Seattleites consider unfurling an umbrella the equivalent of raising a flag that says BOO HOO I'M MELTING. Every time the spoke of my umbrella pokes someone else's umbrella, I feel like when you accidentally brush against someone's breast and aren't sure whether to apologize or pretend it didn't happen.

Finally, we turned off onto an alley that looked like a wrong turn. Becky has already explained how, all over Tokyo, you can take a few steps off a main street of ten-story neon and onto a pedestrian path or a residential cloister. It's like a *Twilight Zone* scene where time stops and everything goes silent, except for the protagonist.

Your protagonists walked a few feet down the alley and into Chachakōbō. What do I love about this place?

- Not a lot of cafes in Tokyo focus on Japanese tea. (This is true, I swear.) This one does, and it's totally unpretentious about it.

- The name is fun to say. The macrons over the O's mean "hold that syllable and round your lips like you're working up to a kiss." If you don't feel silly, you're saying it wrong.

- From the perspective of Toll House cookie- and sundae-munching Westerners, they serve the most improbable desserts.

The desserts at Chachakōbō are actually quite normal by Japanese standards. Red bean paste is the most quintessential ingredient for Japanese sweets. Becky is normal for loving it; I'm the weird one. Another dessert served at the cafe is *oshiruko,* hot red bean soup. I did try a bite of the matcha cream anmitsu to confirm that this isn't my kind of thing. It's not, but it is lovely, and I applaud the theory: It's dessert! Let's combine as many unusual textures as possible!

The agar chunks forming the base of the anmitsu remind me of the contents of a silica gel package that got water splashed on it. Or, I hesitate to bring this up, but have you ever torn open a (clean) disposable diaper and seen the absorbent beads inside? Kind of like that, but chunkier.

Now, let's talk about tea. I think it would be a damn shame to go to Japan and not drink some really good tea, and this is an excellent place to do it. Chachakōbō serves both sencha (brewed tea) and matcha (powdered tea, whipped to a froth with a bamboo whisk). The menu is in Japanese, but with illustrations, and it doesn't really matter which tea you order; they're all good.

Your tea will arrive on a tray with four components: a teacup, a teapot, a *yuzamashi* (a secondary pitcher for cooling down the water, because boiling water is too hot for delicate green tea leaves), and a small piece of slippery confectionery. Drink the tea in the cup, then steep it again by pouring the water from the yuzamashi into the pot and letting it steep for 20 to 30 seconds. Pour the second infusion into your cup, shaking the pot to extract the last few drops. There's also a hot water pitcher on the table for a third and maybe fourth infusion. For most teas, the second infusion is quite different from the first, and that's part of the joy of drinking Japanese tea.

We would have hung out at Chachakōbō for hours, but we had an appointment to meet an old friend of mine. So we headed back out into Takadanobaba, blissfully unaware that we'd be swallowing sperm shortly thereafter.

# HERE'S MILT IN YOUR EYE

## MATTHEW

Let me Google something real quick.

*Your search - "economist Milton Friedman fish jizz" - did not match any documents.*

Well, this ground's about to get broken.

Becky and I met up with Shūhei Kitagawa, an econ major at the prestigious Waseda University. Shūhei spent a year in Seattle as an exchange student at University of Washington, my alma mater. We used to meet up once a week for language practice. He thought it was weird at first that I knew all the food words in Japanese and seemingly none of the other words, but he got used to it.

Shūhei spotted me in front of the Don Quijote discount store outside Takadanobaba. We had the awkward reunion of two straight dudes who haven't seen each other in a while, are not sure if they're friends or colleagues, and are meeting up in a different country from where they last parted. This is a recipe for the world's most awkward hug. We went to a nearby branch of the San Marco Café chain to wait for Becky, who was finishing up some shopping.

Like Dominique Ansel's bakery in New York, San Marco Café is known nationwide for one signature product, and it's a peculiar croissant. Ansel's baby is the cronut. San Marco's is the Choco-Cro, a triangle of croissant dough folded around a thick slab of chocolate like a swaddled baby. As a croissant, it's a morsel of mediocrity on par with what you'd get at a supermarket bakery counter. As a piece of junk food, however, it's perfection: soft, warm, and gooey. I didn't buy one on this stop only because I'd had one earlier that day.

Becky found us at the café and we headed for a restaurant Shūhei had picked out. "I've never actually been to this place," he said. "But my friend said it was good. They serve Kyūshū food."

My tongue woke up. Kyūshū is the southernmost of Japan's four main islands, known for pork, blowfish, hot pot dishes (especially involving offal), and many other delicacies. "Kyūshū food" is an overly general term akin to saying "Southern food" in America to encompass everything from Texas barbecue to Cuban food from Miami. As we've already established, it's best to just ignore any red flags, assume a restaurant in Japan is good, and go with it.

Shūhei's friend nailed it. We had an assortment of pickles including silky pickled shiitake caps; a steamer full of tender pork belly, cabbage, and more mushrooms to dip in a rich soy-based sauce; and a Kumamoto specialty called *karashi renkon*, lotus root stuffed with hot mustard, sliced thin, and fried. We drank beer and talked about life in Japan versus America. Shūhei said he was considering grad school in the U.S. "University of Chicago?" I asked, naming the most famous economics department I could think of.

"Never," replied Shūhei. "I hate Milton Friedman."

Fair enough. I scanned the menu for a dish to start the next round and alighted on *shirako*. "Shirako" is literally "white children" in Japanese. This means exactly what you think it means: It's the sperm sac of a fish. Mullet, in this case. In English we call it "soft roe" or "milt," the latter, naturally, an allusion to the Nobel-winning economist.

Anyway, as soon as I saw tempura-fried sperm on the menu, I knew I had to order it, because, well, do I even have to explain? I'd never tried it before. I figured it would be slimy and weird and I'd pretend to like it for the privilege of watching Shūhei and Becky contend with it.

The sperm arrived as golden-brown breaded square packets. I lifted one with my chopsticks and took a bite. The breading was light, crisp, and salty. The contents were white and fluffy, like slightly runny egg whites. I chewed. This stuff was delicious. Like eating a cloud. I rolled it around on my tongue and swallowed. I had many uncomfortable thoughts. Then I went back for another bite.

## BECKY ✿

Prior to walking into Kusudama (which means "Kyūshū Pearl"), all that I knew about izakayas I learned from a 30-minute Japanese TV show on the plane ride over to Tokyo. Obviously, I was an expert by the time we landed. America is certainly no stranger to bars, so what makes Japanese bars different? Izakayas are where everyday folks go to let off some steam, complain about their boss and temporarily relax their business-first, Japanese-style formality. For perspective, Americans "relax our formality" by sending dick pics to our Tinder dates. If you really let it go in America, you'll be redecorating the back alley with a greatest hits of all that you drank earlier and telling the cab driver how much you really, really looooove him. In Japan, it might mean loosening your tie and bowing less deeply. If you end up drinking too much in Japan, your friends will escort you—one on each side, arm-in-arm-in-arm-in-arm—through the train station and safely into your bed. Such restrained drunkenness stands in stark contrast to what typically goes down on a Saturday night in Seattle (if anyone knows that drunk girl straddling a telephone pole on the corner of Pine Street and 11th, you might want to come and get her).

In America, every blue moon you might stumble upon a bar that serves genuinely good and interesting food, but the average menu in most true-blue American drinking holes is inevitably fries, burgers, nachos and buffalo wings. "Fancier" places have jalapeño poppers that are not from a freezer bag. None of these foods are inherently bad, mind you, but you don't go to most bars in America to eat good food. Let's pretend Americans did that and see if it fits:

---

*Location*: Lodi, California
*Establishment*: Hootie's Hurl Hut

"Hey man, let's go to the Hurl to grab some eats, I heard their fish en papillote is slammin'!"

"Duuuude, we can chill, watch the game, do some shots, and share a plate of charred maitake mushrooms and spring onion with yuzu-infused ponzu and then do pull-tabs."

---

I'm not sure who was or was not consulted in the development of American bar culture but it was clearly decided that great food and drinking holes are segregated concepts. Unless of course you think pickled eggs, stale bags of bar chips, and tater tots are haute cuisine. If that's the case, Hootie's Hurl Hut will really surprise you. Highly recommended!

Izakaya cuisine has loftier aspirations than simply being used to hold your liquor down. The Japanese simply refuse to waste a meal to bad food. If you are in an izakaya to socialize, go nuts, or drown your sorrows, your icy cold foamy-headed mugs of Sapporo will most likely be accompanied by dishes as bizarre as tempura fried fish sperm or as delectable and approachable as bamboo-steamed pork and cabbage.

But all of this is beside the point because what you really want to know is, what did the lesbian think of the fish sperm? Well, it wasn't the worst thing I've ever had in my mouth—and, truth be told, I'm going to be looking at male fish a little differently now. Spongy, marshmallowy and encased in a delicate overcoat of tempura batter, it was rich like uni but with a much more delicate flavor and mild ocean brininess. Matthew and I took a bite at the same time and the way we looked at each other—well, it almost left me misty-eyed.

Nothing bonds friends like sharing a mutual mouthload of milt.

# GAY DIPPING NOODLES

## MATTHEW

Before mentioning to Becky that I wanted to take her to my favorite tsukemen restaurant, it hadn't occurred to me that "tsukemen" is pronounced similarly to "it's gay men."

"It's a gay men restaurant?" she said. "What does that even mean?"

"No, tsukemen. Dipping noodles."

"It's gay men dipping noodles? Are we invited?"

We're invited, as long as we're willing to line up. On our last day in Tokyo, I took Becky to Fuunji (FOON-jee), probably my favorite noodle place in the world. I love noodles. I love eating absurdly porky tonkotsu ramen, cold soba at a standing-only joint in the basement of Shinjuku station, curry udon, Thai rice noodles, Korean...I could literally go on like this all day. I hope the devil never comes out of his lair at AEON Mall and forces me to choose between my family and noodles.

What makes Fuunji so great? The fact that you have to line up and wait until you're starving probably has something to do with it. Luckily, when we arrived at the place around lunchtime, the line was surprisingly short, only a few stylish but somehow nerdy guys queuing patiently. (Japan was full of nattily-dressed nerds long before the startup-infested neighborhoods of urban America.) As soon as we took our place in line, however, a man politely pointed out that we were cutting: the line continued behind us, with a gap to allow pedestrians to pass freely. Not only that, the restaurant had hung a paper sign with a hand-drawn diagram showing how to line up properly.

Becky and I apologized and went to the back of the line. We felt so much better a few minutes later when a Japanese guy committed the same faux pas.

The line at Fuunji moves fast, because the restaurant operates according to an unwritten Soup Nazi-esque code. You enter the restaurant, which seats about sixteen, all at a low counter. To the right is the ticket machine. The special tsukemen, which is what you want, is 1000 yen. You insert the cash, collect your ticket, and get back in line. In an only-in-Japan arrangement, the line continues down the cramped space behind the seated diners. As those poor saps are trying to enjoy their noodles, you're literally breathing down their necks, slavering after their seats.

Finally, you reach the end of the counter and hand your ticket to a staff member, who will ask how large a portion of noodles you want. You can choose from *nami* (regular) or *ōmori* (large). They're the same price. Get the regular. The staff directs you to your seat, and your noodles will arrive moments later. The food is prepared by a team that includes a guy whose massive coif suggests that he's getting plenty of collagen in his diet.

Is it gay men dipping noodles? You will never know, because Fuunji couldn't be less conducive to romance, people-watching, conversation, or any other form of human interaction. And that's part of what makes it so great. Once the noodles arrive, an invisible clock starts. It's you vs. food. You want to eat while the dipping broth is still hot, and then give up your seat fast for the next patron. It's good karma.

Remember when we were dipping cold soba in sauce at Soba Daian? Tsukemen is a new dish inspired by that old way of eating soba. People in Tokyo talk about the "tsukemen boom" of the early 2000s, but it remains popular. It's kind of like how everyone was talking about kale or Korean tacos or molecular gastronomy for a few months, and those things didn't go away.

Tsukemen noodles are fat wheat noodles—not as thick as udon, but close—served cold on a plate. The sauce is thick enough to stick a fork in, a heavily reduced meat stock loaded with savory bits: braised pork chunks, bamboo shoots, nori, and a soft-cooked egg. Just before serving, the cook spoons a brownish powder on top of a little seaweed. The powder is *gyofun,* pulverized dried fish. Stir it in for extra umami.

Get to work, pilgrim. Pick up a few noodles with

your chopsticks, dip them in the sauce, bring them to your mouth, and...

... MY TRAINING IS COMPLETE.
... I AM READY.

THE WILL IS STRONG ...
THE BODY IS PREPARED ...
WE SHALL SHOW NO FEAR!

LET'S GO!
SLURRRRRP
SLURRRRRP
SLURRRRRP

## BECKY ✿

...and suddenly you're Takeru Kobayashi, the famous competitive eater, except it's not Twinkies or hot dogs or meatballs, it's tsukemen and it's fabulous and everyone wants to be where you are because you've waited a while to get there and you're being shuttled in the door, one by one, hungry automatons, shuffling forward inch by inch, and you're breathing down the neck of the people who will soon, so soon, vacate their seats so you can occupy them. No, own them. And you're breathless and excited and you've been waiting for this moment for at least 42, 43 minutes. The slurping is stereophonic. The unending click-clacking of chopsticks on plates of ice cold wheat noodles provides a repetitive and discordant note that I think Philip Glass would find pleasing. People are eating, people are leaving, people are sitting. The seats are almost never liberated from the bottoms of the eaters. The salty, rich umami-licious pork gravy at Fuunji will cool long before the seats at Fuunji ever will.

Just think about that for a second.

Think about the temperature of the seats in a restaurant and how it might correlate to the numbers of people lining up down the street. You with me now? Forget Yelp; if you want to know how good a restaurant is, simply sit down. Cold seat? The food must surely suck. Get up and leave before you contribute a misleadingly positive review. Wiggling, uncomfortably hot seat? Whoops, someone's still there. Apologize. Warm seat? Just right. The food is great.

When it was our turn and we were shimmying

down the line towards the just barely vacated seats, I felt nervous. I might as well have been on the edge of a pool, my speedo on, my left foot behind me, right foot pointed forward, my hands grabbing the starting block. The whistle blows and Matthew is dead to me and I am dead to him. It's a race to the bottom of the plate and bowl. Which, to be clear, is not really how I prefer to eat. I'm a slow eater, more contemplative Buddhist than Dyson-powered noodle sucker. The more I like the food, the slower I like to eat. But I'm also someone easily influenced by the environment around me and this was Olympic noodle eating and if the job required me to morph into Mark Spitz or Amy Van Dyken or Misty Hyman (holy Christ, who is naming these swimmers anyhow?) then I will adapt, tie my bib on, channel Joey "Jaws" Chestnut, pound some damn noodles and swim through hellfire or gravy to victory.

# IT'S A WRAP

## BECKY ✿

A while back I shared with Matthew a concept he mentioned in his book *Pretty Good Number One.* I call it Vacation Head, and it postulates that whatever you experience on vacation will inevitably kick the ass of anything at home, just by virtue of the fact that you are in a completely different head space on vacation. It's in full effect when you hear people gush "OMG, Teresa! The chicken yakitori in Tokyo was the best thing I've had in my mouth my whole life." Except, no, Teresa, seriously, it really was. And while Vacation Head is certainly a legitimate condition, noted in the DSM-IV under Delusions, the food really is better in Japan. Not that I can't find great Japanese food in Seattle from time to time, but the gaps in consistency are always lingering above the experience.

I even learned something about human interaction that had nothing to do with food. Unless I directly sought help from a Tokyoite or accidentally bumped into someone, people didn't make eye contact or smile when passing on the street. Admittedly, smiling into the face of everyone at Shibuya crossing would be exhausting, if not impossible. However, the head down, eyes-in-front policy continued onto the quiet streets. In Seattle, not necessarily an unfriendly place, I say good morning to people I pass on these quieter streets, or at least offer a hedge-my-bets closed-mouth smile. My attempt at urban friendliness is often returned with an emotionless stare, which tends to diminish my daily happiness quotient. Since coming home, I've changed the way I spend my emotional currency, saving it up for actual one-on-one interactions. Thanks, Tokyo: I will be adding the concept of The Conservation of Friendliness to my list of made-up travel-related syndromes, along with Vacation Head.

I don't want you to think I'm so totally in love with Tokyo that I'm not aware of its problems. For example, I bet there are criminals here. I'm sure there are shitty cooks and parts of the city that are disgustingly unclean. It's just that I never met any criminals or shitty cooks or saw any litter. And we went all over the city; we were in suburban, urban, touristy and business districts and across all of them we never encountered any of these things.

In conclusion, while it pains me to write this (because Matthew is like the little brother I never wanted but after awhile have grown attached to like a friendly callus) he's absolutely right about everything he ever told me about Japan.

A trip to this city deserves all the accolades I can muster. Tokyo, you haven't seen the last of me.

## MATTHEW

If there's one thing about Japan I hate (other than the summer weather and smoking in restaurants), it's the Narita Express.

The Narita Express is a train that runs to and from Narita Airport. There's almost nothing interesting about it. Coming from the airport, at Tokyo Station it splits into two trains, like a worm that regenerates if you cut it in half. This bifurcation is shown on an LCD display in each train car, but you can't actually feel it. (It would be great if they figured out a way to split a car in half right between a couple of rows of seats, without killing any passengers except for some guy talking loudly on his phone.)

On the way back to the airport, the two six-car trains fuse into a single twelve-car train and head out through Chiba, past the SkyTree, to the airport. Narita International Airport is really far from Tokyo. From the west side of town, where we stayed, it's about fifty miles, and the train takes ninety minutes. By American standards, the Narita Express is a high-speed train; by Japanese standards, it's slower than the lines at Tokyo Disney.

Every time I get on the Narita Express heading for the airport, I have the same thought: I don't have to get on this train. I could just stay here until I run my checking account down to zero or they arrest me for overstaying my visa. And then I wimp out, and spend ninety boring minutes on the train thinking about all the things in Tokyo I'll miss. Chain restaurants with amazing food. Soy milk lattes worth drinking. Intricate packaging. TV commercials on trains. Convenience store rice balls. Reading a menu and feeling like a kid who just learned to read. I even miss things I don't care about, like stationery, cat cafés, and tiny neighborhood temples.

The Japan strain of Vacation Head is a communicable disease. Now that Becky and I are both afflicted, we're giving it to you. Go to Tokyo. Find an apartment on Airbnb and stay in a neighborhood not mentioned in your guidebook (we stayed in Takadanobaba, but I'm also fond of Nakano, Kōenji, Kichijōji, and Jiyūgaoka). Wander around, go into a random restaurant, and point at stuff. Ride on trains. We've included a list of the places we went, but just go and get lost. See you if and when you get back.

# ONE YEAR LATER . . .

# 小さい鳥
# LITTLE BIRD

## BECKY ✿

### DAY 1

It's one thing to travel to a foreign country you've never been to with a friend who has been there four times previously. It's another thing entirely to be the tour leader to your spouse with only one trip under your crappily-tied *obi.* Matthew and his family were planning to join us, but life got in the way and they couldn't make it.

"You'll be fine!" Matthew assured me. "And I need you to do something important."

"Anything, what?" I asked.

"Bring us all the weird Hi-Chew flavors you find."

Oh, easy, I told him. I'm on it.

But first we had to get to Tokyo, stand in a long line representing all the colors of the international rainbow, walk through customs, exchange our cash, and figure out how to drag our jet-lagged bodies to the hotel. I tried to set myself up for success while I was in Seattle planning our arrival. "Don't be a hero," I told future me (future me is often an asshole). "You don't need to show off to your wife how much you know about Tokyo. She already married you and knows you're full of shit. Get through customs and stay in an airport hotel that first night. Get your bearings. You're a little bird—hop, don't try to fly."

We locate our bags, exchange our cash, ask for help when the Pasmo transportation card machine outsmarts us, and follow the signs to what we think will be a shuttle to our airport hotel. Wrong. Right there, a stone's throw from baggage claim, is the formal entrance to our hotel. It's midnight and very quiet in the airport. The hotel workers wave us in and greet us with deep bows; a porter sweeps in to take our bags; and a friendly man presents us with an envelope that says SELENGUT-SAN on it: our pre-ordered SIM cards for our phones. The porter leads us up to our room. Out of habit I reach for a tip and then remember that tipping is just not done in Japan.

If you remember, Matthew had only one thing to say about airport hotels: that they are only good for convention hook-ups. With low expectations, we open the door. It smells fresh and clean. It's modern—stylish even—and so close to baggage claim that a person could get shit-faced on mini-bar bottles and then pop down to take joy rides on the conveyor belts. Hypothetically.

Exhausted and hungry, we climb into bed, scan the room service menu, and place our order. Thirty minutes later, we hear a knock at the door and are greeted by a room service attendant. He wheels the cart into the room and with an air of formality and professionalism lifts the silver tray off of the platter, revealing a sushi selection more beautiful and pristine than most of the food in your average American sushi bar. Minutes later, I look over at April, a perfect piece of wild salmon nigiri on her chopsticks.

"Wow," she says. "Just wow."

## DAY 2

One thing I notice immediately about traveling with April is that every time she says something about how awesome Japan is, I smile and nod and act like she's complimenting me. "Right? *Right?*" I say. Such a strange bit of egotism to feel personally thanked on behalf of a nation that you just happened to visit first. Now I understand that strange smirk and phantom mic-drop Matthew did each time I went gaga over some tiny awesome thing I saw when we walked the streets together. It just feels good when someone you love—or perhaps in Matthew's case, tolerates—appreciates what you appreciate.

My primary concern is to relax and enjoy Tokyo with my wife, but my mission, one I'm taking frighteningly seriously, is to scour this city of approximately 7,000 convenience stores for any Hi-Chew flavor other than grape, strawberry, green apple, cherry, peach, banana, lemon, or mango. It seemed like an easy enough promise to make back in Seattle, but now, on the morning of our first full day in Tokyo, standing in front of a bewildering array of colors and candy names written in kana, I remember I'm not so great at reading yet. "Right here!" I yell to April, and then realize it's a totally different brand of candy, packaged nearly identically to Hi-Chew, which is sort of like saying that the word "Oreos" looks annoyingly like "Chips Ahoy!"

We grab a snack of *onigiri* (rice balls) and April heads off down the street eating it before I grab her arm and try not to sound totally douchey as I explain, "They just don't do that here." The Japanese stand and eat at designated areas just outside the convenience stores or at the vending machines. Walking while eating, drinking, or smoking is frowned upon. We finish our snack and April balls up her trash and—total rookie move—starts looking for a garbage can. It's shocking how clean Tokyo is when you consider that there are perhaps four garbage cans in the entire city. Apparently, people carry their own plastic trash bags with them, sorting their trash throughout the day as they accumulate it and then bringing it home to their city-enforced domestic Draconian trash system.

We hit two more stores looking for Hi-Chew—bubkes—and refocus our day on navigating ourselves and our luggage through the subway to the same exact ryokan that I stayed at with Matthew, Ryokan Shigetsu, located in the historic neighborhood of Asakusa. Just outside Sensō-ji, Asakusa's famous Buddhist temple, we discover the impossible: the only bad food in Tokyo. We notice a street fair going on, and just like that yakitori place Matthew and I went to last year, it's giving us all the classic signs of potentially bad food. Matthew taught me over and over again to ignore signs like an empty restaurant with a million things on the menu. I extrapolate the theory to fair food: Hot dogs, strange-smelling things on skewers, lines of children holding blow-up animals on sticks—all the schlock one might expect. The smell is a little off, but it's Tokyo and all the food is amazing here, so I home right in on a violently colored skewer of meat. The color is a Benjamin Moore speciality blend of Fake Tan orange and Flaming Blood Sunset. The meat is actually fish. Or rather, Krab. Still, I buy it. April chooses a hot dog. They're both equally, repulsively horrible and taste remarkably similar. As easily as I took the compliments for Tokyo, I'm defending its honor to April, "This is a complete anomaly," I hedge. "Probably a foreign contractor."

"Well," April says, "I mean, it's fair food, I didn't expect it to be great." Which is an entirely reasonable thing to say, but then I start getting grumpy because—work with me, Japan—I've been building you up for months now and I thought you were perfect and now I'm dumping Mr. Krab Stick into—what is that? It's one of the four garbage cans in this city.

It turns out, Matthew, that you can ignore all the signs of bad food until that one day when you can't. When I tell him about the horrible fair food, he says, completely unsurprised, "Oh, yeah, hot dogs in Japan are universally disgusting. I have no idea why."

## DAY 3

We're at the hospital. No, I didn't get listeria from Mr. Krab Stick. We're here to meet the new baby our friends Luuvu and Mikiko just had. Getting here was half the fun and involved a mime routine to two oblivious strangers on the Saint Luke's campus where I aggressively bounced a baby in my arms while April made cry faces followed by tall building gestures. The kind strangers pointed behind us to the clearly marked sign that said, in English, "Birth Center."

Here is the good news about having a baby in Japan: You get to stay in the hospital for five days and the hospital food rocks. On the second or third day, when the new mom's appetite has returned, the hospital sends a congratulatory meal. Google image search "oiwaizen" (celebratory food) and you'll get a good sense of the beauty and care that goes into this special meal. Mikiko's oiwaizen was served on large lacquered black trays and featured a whole grilled red sea bream; a so-called "angel" prawn, nearly four inches long and still in its shell; maitake mushroom soup; tofu; stewed pork belly; festive rice and red beans; and pickled carrots and daikon (the colors red—or orange in this case—and white are celebratory and often used for weddings and births). We weren't actually there to see this special meal, but Mikiko's sister Chiaki texted me a photo of it and said it was every bit as good as restaurant food. Hospital food in Japan is so good, they probably just call it "food."

We grab the others and leave Mikiko so she can get some rest and head to Gyu-Maru, located under the

Ginza line train tracks in a new complex called Yūrakuchō Sanchoku Inshokugai ("Yūrakuchō neighborhood farm-fresh food and drink"). It's a raucous scene, tables pushed close together, a tunnel of laughing heads, chopsticks, bubblegum J-pop blaring through the speakers. Customers shout "Suu-mii-ma-sen!!", arms hyperextended, to grab the waiters' attention. Beer, sake, whisky, and highball mixtures of Shochu and soda are being passed around. A rowdy group of Australian men at the table to our left exchange toasts with us. A young Japanese woman is sitting just behind us wearing a shirt that boldly declares in black block letters: PERVERT. Purposeful statement or cool English word that has no meaning for the wearer? Unclear.

Food arrives in waves through a haze of cigarette smoke, hands grab trays, and there is never enough room on the table for all the food Chiaki is ordering. At this complex, all the restaurants are under the same management, so you can order from the restaurant you're actually sitting at or one nearby. We get *fugu* (blowfish) from the fish place and horse sashimi from Umakabai Delicious Horseflesh. The horse meat is divided on the plate into various cuts.

"What is that?" I ask Chiaki, pointing to some fatty looking yellowish-white slices of meat, in stark contrast to the rest of the meat which resembles raw beef.

"Oh, that's the mane."

I pretend I don't know what that word means even though it's in English, take a bite, and keep chewing. The mane is a slick, fatty, water-balloon-like foreign object in my mouth, filling with my saliva, doubling in size despite my now-vigorous attempts to make it go down. I press my hands on the table to ground myself for forceful chewing. Our table is a slab of wood nailed precariously onto stacks of Asahi beer crates. It's groaning from the weight of the dishes and my stress-chewing. There's a TV blaring ads, deafening music and talking, dishes being scraped and loaded into a dishwasher, crashing beers *kampai*-ing together: It's total chaos and we are loving it. I can't hear myself think, which is a good thing, because what I'm thinking is, *Oh my god, I'm eating THE BLACK STALLION.*

## DAY 4

I'm concerned about April. I think she has some rare form of international pica, because on every one of our trips she identifies the local version of ice-based desserts and leads us on a death march to find the best one. In Hawaii I had to limit her to three shave ice a day because her lips turned blue—from the artificial dye or the cold, I wasn't sure. It's October in Japan, and thank god it's not the right season here. Her Japanese is rudimentary, but she's nailed down the word for shave ice (*kakigōri*) and she's saying it with authority. Even though there are hardly any places selling it right now, April manages to find it three times. Today. Breakfast is peach kakigōri, with ripples of paper-thin real peach curled throughout. We just happen upon the stand in Asakusa, not far from where we're staying. We eat outside at their only table: one cup, two spoons. Lunch is in Roppongi at Yelo (open year-round for any addicts in your life), a matcha-flavored kakigōri for me with red azuki beans and a white Afro of frozen sweet milk on top; a garishly colored, seasonally-appropriate pumpkin ice for April. Dinner is strawberry ice for April and more matcha for me at a hole-in-the-wall Turkish restaurant that makes it on the side, a mash-up of cultural menu offerings that my tweaking spouse appreciates.

Kakigōri, besides being incredibly fun to say, is notably different from Hawaiian shave ice in the flavors offered and in the textural differences. It's closer to Filipino halo halo, with the milk and beans (thank god no canned corn) but uniquely its own thing. The best stands and stores proudly display the provenance of the ice (water from the slopes of Mt. Fuji, anyone?).

Between hits of kakigōri, we window shop and come upon an unfortunate advert for a paper manufacturing company on the side of a building that says "Feel Wood!" These not-quite-right translations are a huge source of entertainment. April and I burst out laughing at the scandalously named bar: 10-Sluts, and then take selfies in front of it. We crack up at an instant coffee in a can called Morning Shot, and laugh nervously at a well-intended ad for Fair Trade imported art that features smiling Guatemalan women with the words "Happy Trade, Happy Ethnic!" plastered above their faces.

We step into our new favorite store Don Quijote, or Donki for short. Donki sells a riotous grab bag of crap in a total sensory-overload multi-storied skinny building. Matthew has a panic attack just thinking about the place so I didn't get to go in on my last trip. April and I can't get enough Donki. It reminds me of Chubby and Tubby, the iconic cheap goods store in Seattle that closed years ago, where you could buy shoes, $5 Christmas trees, kitchen goods, pellet guns, and a wheelbarrow. April and I keep running after each other holding up random things (cat ears! Hello Kitty headphones!) The Japanese are insanely pro-Halloween and every store is decorated to the hilt. Halloween costumes come with hilarious names, like a Michael Jackson mask branded "Play Thing." Or the cringe-worthy "Black Maid," the kind of costume a fraternity brother would wear at a rager just before the university revokes his frat's charter.

On the way out of Donki, I see a kit for making your very own miniature kakigōri stand and decide that I cannot leave this country without purchasing this very unique thing (a common vacation move, and about as advisable as buying a mini-tandoor in India or 10 brightly colored sarongs in Thailand that you swear you'll wear back home in Ohio). We add it to our basket along with kabocha squash–flavored Kit-Kats, a set of Hello Kitty shot glasses, and what I think is a great deal on chef aprons, only to find out later in our apartment that I have just purchased three miniature and theoretically sexy black "aprons" that might cover half of my junk in calm wind conditions. I leave them in our apartment in Nakano with a note that says, "Oops! Maybe you can use?" Who is the "you" in this note? Probably not Makoto, the kind man who is the property manager of our rental apartment, but who am I to assume?

## DAY 5

I've lost my cell phone. I left it in a Tokyo Starbucks this morning, and the embarrassing bit is that I'm not entirely sure which Starbucks because we went to two today. Why, you might be asking, would we hang out in Starbucks when we live in Seattle? I went in purely for one reason, and that was to see if they'd spell my name wrong on my cup just like they do back home. But then I remember I can't really read Japanese, so it might say Bucky, as it once did at a Seattle Starbucks, or it might say "Happy Ethnic!" Also, I'm lying. I went to two Starbucks today because they have free Wi-Fi (something surprisingly hard to find in tech-savvy Tokyo) and those *hōjicha* (roasted green tea) lattes Matthew got me addicted to last year.

We walk back into the Ginza district Starbucks (fun fact: it's the very first Starbucks in Tokyo) and ask if anyone turned in a cell phone. What I probably say is "phone help excuse me" and after some polite bowing and confusion, the kind Starbucks worker shakes his head and makes an "x" with his arms (a very Japanese gesture for "no, sorry"). Time to head across town to the other Starbucks. April is remarkably patient with me considering I have a storied career of losing important shit. Amazingly, these lost items almost always boomerang back to me (a stolen guitar recovered by the Seattle police, a wallet returned two years later, a computer). We walk into the second Starbucks and I head straight to the counter, "Sumimasen," I stammer. "iPhone?" The woman smiles broadly, runs into the back, and returns in a moment with my phone, which she hands over with two hands and a deep bow. I bow back, deeper, and thank her effusively. April shakes her head.

It's pouring outside and wall-to-wall packed in here. We step first to one side and then back to the other to avoid customers lining up for coffees, and locate a plug so I can make sure this is actually my phone. I bend over to plug the phone in and my hip smacks my umbrella and it clatters over, sliding down the wall and into the legs of an elderly couple seated next to us. I pick it up, apologize and lean it up against the wall, where it slides right back down and into the legs of the couple. April is moving quickly away from me. Suddenly the employee who gave us the phone appears in front of me carrying a tray with two hot beverages on it and she is smiling at me and saying things I don't understand. I'm so in the way, so supersized, so unsure of what she is asking of me. *Oh!* I think, *perhaps she is offering us these hot beverages, a celebration of reuniting us with our phone. Japan is amazing!* I take the drinks off the tray, and the elderly couple stares at me and starts waving their hands. I hand the drinks back to the employee, rip my phone out of the wall, and beat a path to the door.

My umbrella clatters to the floor, abandoned.

## DAY 6

We happen to be in Tokyo the same week our friend Luuvu—yes, the same one who just had a new baby—is hosting the grand opening party for his new food truck company called Mobile Canteen. He has two trucks in his fleet, one called Melt (where he tests out new concepts on the public) and the other +84, his banh mi and Vietnamese coffee truck, inspired by his childhood in Vietnam. His party is also part of the Aosandō Art Fair, and April and I meet up with Chiaki to help him celebrate.

The food truck scene in Tokyo is growing, and is a great way to explore other food cultures in a city dominated by Japanese cuisine. The trucks converge on outdoor festivals and sporting events or sometimes rent space in front of other businesses for more permanent digs. Tokyo food trucks are tiny and cute. Sure, there's a practical reason for this: They need to fit into tight spaces. But it's hard not to think of the diminutive and adorably decorated micro-vans as just another stop on the continuum of cute that is a hallmark of modern Japanese culture. When more than three gather, they look as intimidating as a convoy of ice cream carts rumbling up to the starting line of a Hot Wheels race track.

We show up to the Art Fair and Luuvu's micro-trucks are parked across from one another, lines snaking back and forth. He's all alone in his truck, understaffed and in the weeds. I call out to him, "Hey, want some help?" He hems and haws for a moment and then nods his head. I run around to the back of the van, duck my head through the micro-door, wash my hands, and pop in beside him. The next two hours are a blur of banh mi assemblage and hot, sweet, coffee. I spread homemade pâté on a warm baguette, layer in sliced pork, ham, pickled daikon and carrots, and pass it over to Luuvu. He adds hot sauce and cilantro, wraps the sandwich in parchment paper and ties it with red and white striped string, and hands it through the window to his worker, who passes it to the customer with a cheery "hai, douzo!" (here you go!). "Arigatō gozaimasu!" (thank you very much) is sung out again and again. An elderly Japanese woman motions to me and when I turn to her, she smiles and points at her sandwich: "Oishii!" (delicious!). I beam with pride. It's not my food or my food truck, and it doesn't matter one bit.

We sell out of sandwiches and I turn to Luuvu. "What time do you want me here tomorrow?"

## DAY 7

Matthew gets really excited to teach me new things about Japan, and he gets the opportunity nearly every day. He began studying Japanese and all things Japan a few years before I did, and it seems that he will forever be my teacher and guide. I'm comfortable with my role as his student, after all, he's got an entire writing system on me that I have not yet learned (kanji, with its 2000-plus characters) and three more trips to Tokyo.

Today I text him about the great izakaya only four blocks from the apartment April and I are renting in Nakano (the exact same building in the exact same neighborhood where Matthew and his family have stayed previously).

"Wait, which izakaya?" he texts, and I immediately think he's setting me up for a teacher moment of some sort.

"Ranman," I reply, "you know, that incredible place

right by 'our' apartment, widely written up."

No response, so I keep typing, "Michelin-rated so-called 'Bib Gourmand' for great food for not much money."

Crickets.

"The place that serves *sanma* (Pacific saury), that luscious seasonal fish, really pointy, amazing with purple shiso flowers on top? Mom-and-pop place, very traditional, no English menu, no smoking, high on quality food, low on typical izakaya chaos?"

I see the ellipses of a potential text. It teeters there for a minute and then goes away.

"We ordered their signature dish of *yuba* (tofu skin) rolls filled with mountain vegetables. Oh, and *kohada,* that little silver fish, lightly pickled, so delicious." I go on and on, telling him about the exquisite service, the elderly couple next to us that helped us navigate the menu, the gentle way the mom (of the mom-and-pop) placed our shoes at the edge of our seating area, the feeling of history and timelessness in the space.

"Wait, it's not new?" he texts.

"75 years new," I reply.

You know what's more delicious than the food at Ranman? Finding something amazing in Tokyo, a stone's throw from Matthew's apartment, that he knows absolutely nothing about.

## DAY 8

Toru Arai, President
Morinaga & Co., Ltd.

2F, Morinaga Plaza Bldg, 5-33-1, Shiba
Minato-ku, Tokyo 101-8403

Dear Arai-sama:

I had one job, and I failed. Or rather, you failed me.

The only flavor of Hi-Chew I have found in all of Tokyo that is remotely exciting to an American fan is acerola cherry—and of course Matthew has already had it before. I've heard your company releases novel flavors based on regional specialities such as white peach, dragonfruit, durian, camu camu berry, ume plum, and bitter orange. Over 100 different flavors, they say. I saw six.

It seems silly that I should focus so much attention on your candy but I felt it was the least I could do to thank Matthew for all his help and guidance. It's not that I don't like your product; I really do, even though most of the time I'm not sure if it's gum or candy, and it has the consistency of a pencil eraser. While reading about your company's history, I learned that in 2008 you recalled some of your products due to complaints that rubber-like material had been found in the candy. An investigation determined that a piece of a worker's glove got into the production line. What's curious to me is that anyone noticed a rubber glove in a candy that has the consistency of a rubber glove.

One might quibble over the texture, but your commitment to regionality and unique flavors sets your company apart from industrial American candy companies. Whereas we have some fake "strawberry" flavor made in a test tube, you combine the flavors of two distinct types of Japanese strawberries (the Tochiotome and Camarosa cultivars). You even have adult-oriented flavors based on the juice of wine grapes. Cabernet Hi-Chew anyone? Chardonnay? Shit, the closest we get to candy that displays regional pride is when Skittles dyed their candy blue and green for the Seahawks. As you might assume, blue tasted exactly like green.

I tried really hard to find the special ones for Matthew, Laurie, and Iris. I'm afraid I'm coming home empty-handed. Well, not completely empty-handed. My extensive web searches for "Hi-Chew Tokyo flavors exotic" led me to this fun fact from Wikipedia: "As the main ingredients (of Hi-Chew) are glycogen and palm kernel oil, it is relatively simple to remove if it becomes stuck on clothing. By applying a warm, wet towel, the candy will soften and wash off."

Thanks, Internet! I'm going to smush this Acerola Cherry Hi-Chew into Matthew's shirt and then teach him how to remove it.

Sincerely,<br>
Becky Selengut<br>
Seattle, Washington

P.S.: Seriously, Morinaga & Co? Why didn't you tell me that they sell all the flavors, arranged by region, at Tokyo Station? My friend Chiaki sent me a photo as proof. She was killing time waiting for her train and there they all were, making a mockery of my fruitless search. Flavors like Amaou Strawberry, Dekopon Orange, and Yubari Melon. Why would you hide your melon, Morinaga? Why? I'm really mad—but not so mad I would turn down a regional flavor gift box if you want to win back my loyalty.

# GLOSSARY

**Agar:** a vegetarian gelatin-like substance with a bouncy texture, popular in desserts and drinks and available in a variety of flavors

**Anago:** saltwater eel

**Anmitsu:** A texture-intensive dessert made with agar and red bean paste, often topped with peas, mochi, and fruit. Matthew's worst nightmare.

**Arigatō gozaimasu:** thank you very much

**Azuki beans:** similar to kidney beans, but eaten most often as dessert, either whole in syrup or as a sweetened paste

**Bento:** boxed lunch containing rice and other dishes, usually in multiple compartments, available at convenience stores, train stations, and (pro tip for the hungry traveler!) in the backpacks of kids you pass on the street

**Bitaazu:** bitters

**Chawanmushi:** steamed savory egg custard

**Chirashizushi:** literally "scattered sushi," a bowl of sushi rice with toppings such as fish, egg, and fish eggs scattered on top

**Daigaku imo:** literally "college potatoes," a glazed sweet potato dish

**Daikon:** A big white radish, used picked, grated, stir-fried, stewed. The taste of cooked daikon is mild, but the smell can clear a stadium.

**Depachika:** the food emporium located in the basement of a Japanese department store, where Becky wants to go to die

**Dōzo:** "here you go" or "please go ahead"

**Gomadōfu:** like tofu, but made with sesame paste instead of soy milk

**Gyofun:** powdered dried fish; an umami bomb

**Hijiki:** brown sea vegetable

**Hōjicha:** roasted green tea

**Hi-Chew:** A taffy-like confection uncomfortably straddling the line between gum and candy. Comes in over a hundred different flavors or six.

**Izakaya:** A bar or pub. Really, just like an American bar, right down to the sashimi you get with your beer.

**Jidori:** popular brand of free-range chicken

**Kampai!:** Cheers!

**Karaage:** fried chicken

**Karashi renkon:** lotus root stuffed with hot mustard

**Kakigōri:** shaved ice

**Kinpira gobō:** burdock, carrot, and hijiki simmered in a sweet soy and sesame sauce

**Kohada:** gizzard shad, commonly served as sashimi or sushi

**Kombu:** kelp

**Koto:** Japanese harp. If you imagine the twangy music that would be playing over tranquil scenes of a Japanese garden, there's probably a koto involved.

**Kyūshū:** the southernmost of Japan's main islands, far from Tokyo, known for hot springs, tonkotsu ramen, offal hot pot, tea, and volcanoes

**Machigaeru:** to make a mistake

**Matcha:** powdered green tea, whipped to a froth with a bamboo whisk

**MegaCock69:** what Matthew seat-to-seat messaged Becky as his ideal "handle" just prior to slumping into an Ambien coma

**Menma:** bamboo shoots

**Nami:** in a restaurant context, refers to a regular-sized dish

**Nigiri (sushi):** Hand-pressed sushi, the kind with a slice of fish on top of a finger of rice. Not to be confused with *American sushi,* the kind with sriracha mayo on top.

**Negi:** a type of green onion; similar to a leek

**Obi:** belt used to tie your *yukata*

**Oden:** a stew of fish cakes and vegetables in a light broth, available at restaurants but also, during colder months, at the front of every convenience store

**Oishii!:** Delicious!

**Okonomiyaki:** a savory pancake made with cabbage, wheat flour, and often pork and seafood

**Onigiri:** A rice ball often shaped into a triangle and stuffed with various ingredients such as ume plum, salmon, or tuna fish. Sold at convenience stores for about a dollar; possibly the best snack on the planet.

**Oshiruko:** sweet red bean soup

**Oyakodon:** chicken-and-egg omelet on rice

**Ōmori:** in a restaurant context, a large-sized dish

**Otsumami:** a small side dish or amuse-bouche served in an izakaya, usually with a nominal cover charge

**Ponzu:** citrus-flavored soy sauce, sometimes with grated daikon, used as a dipping sauce

**Rabu rōshon:** "love lotion" or lubricant

**Ramen:** come on, people, we can only do so much

**Ryokan:** traditional inn

**Sake:** rice wine

**Sanma:** Pacific saury, a type of fish

**Sashimi:** raw fish

**Senbei:** rice crackers

**Sencha:** brewed green tea

**Shabu shabu:** a hot pot dish where meat and vegetables are cooked in clear broth and often dipped in ponzu or another dipping sauce before eating

**Shirako:** literally "white children," refers to the sperm sac of a mullet or other fish

**Shōyu:** the word for soy sauce used by a Japanese person or by a non-Japanese person who thinks they're better than you

**Soba:** buckwheat noodles

**Sobagaki:** a dumpling made from buckwheat flour, often served at soba restaurants

**Sukiyaki:** a hot pot dish of beef, vegetables, soy sauce, and noodles

**Sumibiyaki:** charcoal-grilled

**Sumimasen:** excuse me, sorry, thank you

**Takoyaki:** octopus balls

**Tamagoyaki:** seasoned omelet, traditionally made in a rectangular pan

**Tare:** a concentrated salt- and/or soy-based seasoning sauce

**Tatami:** bamboo sleeping mat

**Tempura:** batter-coated fried food

**Tonjiru:** pork and miso stew

**Tsukemen:** a form of ramen where the eater dips fat wheat noodles into a rich broth

**Tsukemono:** pickled vegetables

**Unagi:** freshwater eel

**Yabai:** Terrible or awesome, depending on the context. (Like how cool kids in America say "bad" when they mean "good." Kids still say that, right?)

**Yakitori:** grilled chicken on sticks

**Yakuza:** Japanese organized crime and the practitioners thereof

**Yuba:** tofu skin

**Yukata:** A light robe worn in summer or at an inn or hot spring. Much easier to put on than a kimono, but foreigners still do it wrong consistently.

**Yuzamashi:** a small pitcher used to cool water when making green tea

**Yuzu:** a type of citrus fruit

# WHERE WE WENT

*For links to more info, visit notoneshrine.com/where*

**Chachakōbō** (Tea, Takadanobaba)
**Chuka Soba Inoue** (Ramen, Tsukiji)
**Don Quijote** (Variety store, many locations)
**Fuunji** (Dipping noodles, Shinjuku)
**Gyu-Maru** at **Yūrakuchō Sanchoku Inshokugai** (Izakaya, Yūrakuchō)
**Isetan** (Depachika, Shinjuku)
**Ishinohana** (Bar, Shibuya)
**Kusudama** (Izakaya, Takadanobaba)
**Mister Donut** (Doughnuts, many locations)
**Miyazaki Nichinan Tsukada Farm** (Chargrilled chicken, many locations)
**Mobile Canteen +84 Banh Mi Truck** (Vietnamese, roving)
**Nagomi Visit** (cooking classes and home visits)
**Papabubble** (Candy, Nakano)

**Ranman** (Izakaya, Nakano)
**Robot Restaurant** (Robots, Shinjuku)
**Ryokan Shigetsu** (Hotel, Asakusa)
**Shinjuku Golden Gai** (Bars, Shinjuku)
**Soba Daian** (Soba)
**St. Luke's Hospital** (Maternity ward, Tsukiji)
**Sumire** (Yakitori, many locations)
**Takashimaya** (Depachika)
**Tenta** (Tempura, Nakano)
**Tsukiji** (Fish market)
**Utsukushii no Yu** (failed onsen attempt, Takaidō)
**Yelo** (Shaved ice, Roppongi)

# IF YOU GO

We tried hard to keep this book as useless as we are, but actual advice kept creeping in. So we're cordoning it off into this section for everyone's safety and including mostly stuff that isn't in every guidebook.

**Rail pass**

If you're going to take multiple or long train trips outside Tokyo, buy a JR Pass (jrpass.com). It's also good on the Yamanote and Chūō lines in Tokyo. If you're just kicking around Tokyo like we did, it's a waste of money.

**Transit card**

So how *do* you get around Tokyo? Buy a Pasmo or Suica card (they're totally equivalent) at any ticket machine (press the English button along the left side first). It's good on every bus and train in Tokyo and many outside Tokyo, and you can reload it at any station. Don't buy paper tickets. You will go insane. Just tap and go. Seriously, we wanted to grab so many confused tourists and give them our cards as a public service.

**SIM card**

If your cell phone provider charges absurd international data rates (and all the American carriers do except for T-Mobile), buy a SIM card. You can order it online and pick it up at the airport or have it delivered to your hotel. We recommend the visitor SIM from b-mobile (http://www.bmobile.ne.jp/english/).

**Getting found**

Google Maps works fantastically well in Tokyo. You can also ask for directions at any police box (Kōban), which are often found on street corners. But if we haven't said this enough already: Spend more time wandering aimlessly than trying to find specific destinations.

**Getting fed**

If you find yourself in a restaurant with no English menu, it's fine to point at other people's food and ask to have that. Or just say "osusume" ("your recommendation") and see what comes out.

**Cooking and culture**

The cooking class we took was offered through Nagomi Visit (https://www.nagomivisit.com/), which also offers home visits where you visit a Japanese family at their home and they make you lunch. Not only is it fun and inexpensive, but you'll probably end up in a part of Tokyo you never would have visited otherwise.

**Learning the language**

Japanese is easy. Just learn all the words in our glossary and you'll be basically fluent.

**No, seriously**

There are tons of good free materials to support your language study, including Anki (http://ankisrs.net/) (flash cards), Human Japanese (http://www.human-japanese.com/) (teaching app), imiwa? (http://www.imiwaapp.com/) (dictionary app), and Mixxer (http://language-exchanges.org/) (Skype-based language partners).

**Movies and TV**

- Anthony Bourdain has visited Tokyo a bunch of times on his various shows (*A Cook's Tour, No Reservations, Parts Unknown*), and all of those episodes are worth seeking out.

- *I'll Have What Phil's Having* is a PBS travel series starring the guy who created *Everybody Loves Raymond.* His first episode covers Tokyo and features Yukari Sakamoto, author of the excellent guidebook *Food Sake Tokyo* (see below). It's on Netflix.

- *Kodoku no Gurume* is a Japanese TV drama series about a businessman who likes to eat alone. There is literally no more to it than that, and it's the most accurate look at casual food in Tokyo we can imagine. You can watch it free online (http://

www.2drama.com/drama/search?key=kodoku&stype=drama) with English subtitles.

### Other books

- *Pretty Good Number One: An American Family Eats Tokyo* (2014) is a book by some guy.
- *Food Sake Tokyo,* by Yukari Sakamoto, covers restaurants, shops, depachika, bars, teahouses, and food vocabulary. Probably you should have read her book before ours. Maybe instead of.
- *Oishinbo* is a long-running comic book series about a cranky, food-obsessed newspaper reporter trying to assemble the Ultimate Menu of Japanese cuisine. Seven volumes have been translated into English and are available where books are sold.

# ACKNOWLEDGMENTS


## MATTHEW

I'd like to thank Becky for letting me invite myself along to Tokyo and for letting me totally punk out on writing that bonus chapter.

Thank you to Akira, Emi, and Mizuki Ohtake for taking me to the mall, which was actually a lot more fun that I made it sound, and for letting me put them in a book *again.*

Without Denise Sakaki's illustrations, this book would be garbage, and she's also a joy to work with. Come on, Denise! A person as talented as you has earned the right to be difficult.

Jill Lightner's editing fixed what was broken, which was a lot. And she's a fellow fan of the Fast & Furious franchise. Ride or die, Jill. Ride or die.

Takuya Hirai and Shūhei Kitagawa each spent a year

helping me improve my Japanese, which is now solidly at first-grade level. I met them through the University of Washington language partner program. If you're studying a language and have a local university, see if they have a similar program. It's free and awesome. Also, Shūhei took us to Kusudama izakaya, home of the crispy fish sperm.

Thanks to Mister Donut, who I like to believe is a real guy.

And, as always, thank you to Laurie and Iris for letting me do my thing, and even encouraging it.

## BECKY ✿

I'd like to remind Matthew that I was the one who invited myself along on his trip to Tokyo, not the other way around. Thank you Matthew for infecting me with your love of all things Japanese. There is no cure, and I am grateful.

Thank you to Luuvu, Mikiko, baby Hiroki, and Chiaki for all the good food, tours, helpful information, translations, and subjecting me to horse mane.

The Japanese Cultural and Community Center of Washington is a great place to learn the language. I thank my teachers and fellow students, and I'll see you again soon—I've heard there's this kanji thing I still need to learn.

Denise Sakaki will always be the coolest and most talented illustrator in the whole world and not just because she drew me my very own Becky avatar. Jill Lightner, you are the most likeable pedant I know. Thank you for kicking my ass and making me a better writer, and please don't edit out the word "pedant."

April, thank you for supporting my new habit and coming with me on a follow-up trip so that you might understand what I've been going on and on about for the last two years. You get it now, right?

## KICKSTARTER BACKERS

This book was made possible by the contributions of 312 backers on Kickstarter, including @WooPigFoodie, Abby Cerquitella, Adam Fulton, Adam Schlesinger, Alex Jomini, Alicea Cole, Allecia Vermillion, Allen Garvin, Allison Day, Allyn Adell Humphreys, Amy Gunther, Amy Koester, Andrea Dunning, Andrew Beck, Andrew Vestal, Angie Neill, Anita Crotty, Ann Venables, Anna Hailey, Anna R Hurwitz, Anna Ring, Anne Pessala, Anonymous (x2), Antonio Campos jr from McAllen TX, Arevra, Ashlyn Forshner, Barcy Fisher and Tina Podlodowski, Beau & Kari Holsberry, Bee family, Ben W Bell, Benson Dastrup, Beth Walsh, Blair Feehan, Bob Pedersen, Brad Mohr, Brenda Vassau, Brian Donaghue, Bruce and Vicki, calcan, Caroline Ferguson, Carrie Carson, Catherine Reynolds, Chris Duval, Cindy Kirtland, Claire Howard, Clare Barboza, Cortney & David, Crystal Sanders aka Baby Mama, Cugurt, Dan Gulden, Dan Shiovitz, Daniel Kramer, Danielle Kramer, Darren Toshi, Darsa Morrow, David Cornelson, David Dadekian, David Fredrickson, David Glasser, David Kudler, David Starner, Dawn Wright, Deanne Katz, Deb Smucker and Liz Wall, Diane M Lee, Donna Adams, Doug Jones,

Eden and Hank Waggoner, Edmonds Bookshop, Elizabeth Clayton, Elizabeth Hale, Elizabeth Holland, Elizabeth Lehner, Emily Short, Erica O'Brien, Erin Foster, esther teodoro, Evelyn Lemon, Fabian 彭 Kärrholm, Fran and Naomi, Gabriel and Kat Claycamp, Glenn, Glenn Austin Green, Gregory Heller, Gunther Schmidl, Heather "not related to Anthony" Weiner, Heather Robinson, Heidi Kenyon, Helen Lee, Henry H Lo, Hsiao-Ching Chou, Isaac 'Will It Work' Dansicker, J. Calligaro, Jack Chan, Jacob "The Shu" Shuster, James A O G Seymour, James Kyoon Yun, Jameson Fink, Janice Granberg, Jason and Hiromi Truesdell, Jason Erickson, Jason Goertz, Jeanne Sauvage, Jen Mosinski, Jennifer Harris, Jennifer Johnson, Jeremy Selengut, Jeroen Burger, Jesse Selengut, Jim Demonakos, Jim Naureckas, Jocelyn, Joe Ray & Elisabeth Eaves, John van Deinse, Jojo Greene, Jon M. Wagner, Judy and Richard Amster, Judy Niver, judy witts francini, Julie Kodama, Julie Whitehorn, Justin de Vesine, Justin Kietzman, Kabian Rendel, Kairu Yao, Kanane Jones, Katherine Malloy, Kathleen Love, Kathleen McDade, Kathy Napolitano, katie dunsmoor, Kelli Cleave, Kelli Garces, Kelvin L Leung, Kevin Abbott, Khris Jackson, Kim & Maxine, Kim and Scott Tennican, Kim B, Kimberly Schaub, Kiran Arain, Kristen & Larry Liang, Kristen Scott, Kylene Abbitt, L. Welfringer, Larry & Meredith Olson, Laura Fulloon, Laura King, Lauren Cascio, Layna & Lawrence, Lee Tostevin, Lia Kawaguchi, Lily Bevis, Lindsay G, Liz Taylor, Liza Daly, Loring Pfeiffer, Luna Brownhurst, Lynda Phan, M Gigi, M Neureuter, M.K. Carroll, Maga4Ever, Maggie Hoffman, Makoto Nagayoshi, Marc Schermerhorn and David Wiley, Marcia Goldberg, Marisa McClellan, Mark & Andrea Frabotta, Mark Roh, Martin Paley, Mary Reilly, Matt Butram and Andrea DelGiudice, Matt Cline, Matt Simmons, Max Elmendorf, Megan DeBell, Mel, Mel Darbyshire, Melinda De Lanoy, Melissa DeWild, Melly, merrily wyman, Michael Burton, Michael Fessler, Michael Sherman and Ed Davis, Michael Wense, Michelle Locke, Michelle Nguyen, Michelle Quigley Pearson, Mike Vrobel, Mikiko Bunn, Milagros L. Wilson, Miles Hunter, Mindy Nass, Nancy Leson, Neil Graham, Neil Robertson, Niels Haverkorn, Nozlee Samadzadeh, Paola Albanesi, Peter Sugarman, Phillip Harris, Porky Bun, Rachel Belle, Rachel M. Grove Rohrbaugh, Rachel Strawn Thibodeaux, Randy Saldinger & Kevin Kelley, Rebecca Staffel, Rebekah Denn, Rebel Powell, Reese Rowe, Renee, Richard E. Morrison, Jr., Robert Musser, Robin Mazna, Robin McWaters, Rolo, Ryan Chan, Ryan Franson, Sally J. Brown, Sarah Barthelow, Scott Heimendinger, Shana Tischaefer, Shannon Cook, Simon Guest, Simon Wistow, Skintight Tamper Bunny and Susan Hautala, Splash, Stacy Cowley, Stefano Morelli, Stephen Johnson, Stesha Brandon, Steve Nicholson, Storme Winfield, SugarPill, Suzannah Kirk, Takoyaki Lightman, Tamara Kaplan, Tami Parr, Tanmeet Sethi, Tara "TJ" Jansson, Teresa, Teresa Engrav, The Laney Family, The Lions, The Pantry, Tieg Zaharia, Tim Heimerle & Rick Lizotte, Tim Hickey, Trevor Grimm, Vivian, Vivienne Dunstan, Wendy Burton, Wendy Richman, and Yuki Caldwell. Thank you so much!

# ABOUT THE AUTHORS

**Becky Selengut** is an author (*Good Fish, Shroom*), private chef, comedy podcast co-host (Look Inside this Book Club), cooking teacher, host of a Youtube cooking channel, cocktail aficionado, and dog wrangler. She lives with her wife April and their two mutts, Izzy and Pippin, in Seattle. She prefers Yamasa brand soy sauce. Find her online at beckyselengut.com.

**Matthew Amster-Burton** writes books and co-hosts a couple of podcasts (including, coincidentally, Look Inside this Book Club). He lives in Seattle with his wife Laurie, daughter Iris, and a cat named Mitaka. Yes, his cat has a Japanese name. He only allows shōyu in his house, never soy sauce. Find him online at rootsandgrubs.com.

CPSIA information can be obtained
at www.ICGtesting.com
Printed in the USA
BVOW03s0253191217
503190BV00001B/18/P